If Only

If Only

The Search for Happiness

Nick Pollard

First published 1999 by Hodder & Stoughton.

This revised and updated edition published 2005 by Authentic
Media, 9 Holdom Avenue, Bletchley,
Milton Keynes, Bucks, MK1 1QR, UK and PO Box 1047,
Waynesboro, GA 30830-2047, USA.

British Library Cataloguing in Publication Data
A catalogue record for this book is available from the British
Library

ISBN 1-90475-305-1

Cover design by fourninezero design.
Print management by Adare Carwin
Printed in Great Britain by Haynes, Sparkford, Yeovil, Somerset

To 'Andy', 'Sharon' and 'Jacqui' (you know who you really are). Thank you for your friendship over the years – and for letting me share some of your life-stories with other people.

Acknowledgements

Thank you to:

- My wife, Carol, and my children, Luke and Lizzie – for your constant support and encouragement
- Catherine Mann, my personal assistant while I was writing the first edition of this book (and Steve Alexander while I was revising it for this edition) – for your patience with me
- Steve Couch, Rachel Bird and the excellent website www.ToolsForTalks.com – for help in updating this second edition
- Jayne Newton for permission to include the lyrics of 'Hope for Today'.
- The very gifted writer, Nick Page – for showing me how to structure a book such as this
- The very gifted actor and writer, Rob Lacey – for helping me to understand the importance of story-telling in philosophy.

Is this a novel? It certainly reads like one. It grips you from the very first page and carries you along at a relentless pace. It is full of surprises and intrigue, of metaphor and imagery. But it is more than a novel – because it is closely based upon true life, most of the characters are real people.

So is it a biography? It certainly helps you to understand the lives of the real characters that you meet in these pages, you seem to live their life and feel their emotions. But it also makes you think about your own life, and about the deeper philosophical questions of human existence.

So is it a book of philosophy? It contains quotes from philosophers past and present – and it certainly helps you to reflect and think at a philosophical level. But this is no dry, dusty text book. Because it reads like a novel . . .

Introduction

The stories you are about to read are based upon true life.
The three main characters are real people. They are
individuals whom I know personally.

However, I have changed their names and many of the
details in the events which I will recount. I have even
made up some other characters and conversations as well
as some scenes and events. I have done this, partly,
because I need to preserve the anonymity of some of these
people. The stories in this book are intensely personal and
two of the main characters have asked specifically that
they should not be identified – for the sake of others in
their lives. I am very happy to comply.

At the end of the day it is not the details of the stories
that are important, but the way in which their experiences
cause us all to reflect upon our own lives. Not many
people who read this book will have had lives like those
described in these pages. But all of us will have known
many of the same thoughts, desires and dreams. Each of
which begin with the same two words – 'If only . . .'

So I appeal to you, don't try to identify the characters in
this book, or try to work out which of the scenes are
exactly true and which have been modified or
constructed. But do let their stories help you to reflect

upon your own life. What are your greatest desires? What do you most want out of this world? What do you think is the meaning and purpose of it all?

I have included sections in the text that are put in italics – these are quotes and stories from philosophers, films and music. I hope that you will find them helpful as you think about the important questions that are raised by the lives of Andy, Sharon and Jacqui.

What is life for? To die? To kill myself at once? No, I'm afraid for that. To wait for death till it comes? I fear that even more. Then I must live, but what for?

Leo Tolstoy (1828–1910)

There must be more to this life – a purpose for us all, a place to belong.

Sarah Jordan, *Beyond Borders* (Mandalay Films, 2003)

1

There are two tragedies in life. One is to lose your heart's desire. The other is to gain it.
George Bernard Shaw (*Man and Superman*, 1903)

Men rise and fall like the winter wheat.
Odysseus, *Troy* (Warner Bros, 2004)

'He's dead.'

'What?' Andy steadied himself against the filing cabinet.

'He's dead. Heart attack or something. We don't know what it is. He just keeled over at his desk.'

'But that's not possible. I've got a meeting with him at lunch-time. We're going over the Wingate report.'

'I'm sorry. He won't be going over anything – with you or with anyone else.'

'Look, quit mucking around. The joke's over. Just get him, will you?'

'Andy, I'm not joking. He really has died. We've called the police. And we're all just sat here looking at him.' The room seemed to become a little dark and the voice faded somewhat into the distance. '. . . Well, to be honest, we are having a bit of a joke at the minute. You've got to laugh, haven't you. What else are you gonna do – cry? He looks so strange lying there. All still. There's some stuff come out of his mouth. But we were just saying how we've all seen that before – when he's had too much Beaujolais or beer – or both. Never exactly one of your health food freaks, was he? But no matter how much he'd had, he was always at his desk. He could certainly put away the booze. I guess that's why he got on so well with you. I remember when . . .'

Andy didn't say anything. He just replaced the phone and sank slowly on to his chair.

'Are you all right?'

'What?'

'A heavy night again, was it?'

'No. Well yes. But . . .' He looked up at his secretary. For once he wasn't the slightest bit interested in the pile of post she carried.

'It's Phillips.'

'Oh no, he hasn't postponed that meeting again has he? Where's he off to now?'

'He's not off anywhere. He's dead.'

'What do you mean "dead"?'

'I mean he's gone, that's it. Look, I need a drink. Just make excuses for me, will you? I want to see if the off-licence is open yet.'

As the doors to the lift closed, Andy stared at his own reflection – blurred and distorted in the metal sheeting. *I reckon that's the third one this month*, he thought to himself. *First there was that guy Jacobs, or something, in accounts. I didn't really know him. He hadn't been here long. Then there was that bloke in the car park. I remember him. I watched as he hit the ground. He'd come to pick up his wife. Pearl, wasn't it? She just had a few more months to go until her retirement. I remember his glasses. After they'd gone in the ambulance, they left them on the ground. They weren't broken, they just didn't take them.*

He shivered a little as he met the cold air in the street. Closing his eyes he breathed in deeply and held it. He stretched his head back as far as it would go and slowly let the air out. In the distance he watched a plane cut the sky with its small white vapour trail.

* * *

British Airways Flight 307 to Sydney, Australia, had taken off about two hours late, and Sharon wasn't happy.

'We were supposed to be in the air by nine o'clock. Three hours we've been waiting in that stupid airport.'

The man sitting next to her made no reply.

'I said we were meant to take off two hours ago.' This time she dug her elbow hard into his forearm as she spoke.

'Look, leave it out will you. Just sit there and shut up.' Tony rubbed his hands up over his face and down again, pulling on his bottom lip and making it stick out like some stroppy school boy. He closed his eyes and tried to lean his head against the frame around the window.

He looked awful. Even Sharon could see that. Tony, the man who could take anything, had taken a bit too much over the last few days. Well, they didn't want to waste it. And they weren't going to take it with them. 'Clean start.' That was what they had both said. They had agreed it together – made a pact.

'In Australia you can . . .' Sharon remembered what the adverts had told them. And that was what they were going to do. Whatever they wanted. Only without the drugs.

Sharon leant across her husband and tried to see the

ground down below. She put her arm on his shoulder and pushed down hard in order to lever herself closer to the window. But Tony wasn't having that. He thumped her in the chest – and she fell back into her seat.

'I'm going to sleep,' he snapped. 'Just leave me alone.'

She had to admit, it wasn't a bad idea. They hadn't exactly slept much last night. And there wasn't really anything else to do until the drinks trolley came around. So she, too, closed her eyes. And tried not to move.

* * *

Ever since I was eleven years old I always found it very difficult to get off to sleep. It was OK before. But not once we had moved down south. I guess it was waiting for the noises to start. When I was younger I suppose I just slept through them. I didn't realise what was happening. Of course I was often puzzled in the morning, when there were no bowls for us to use, or the door was off its hinges. But no-one said anything about it. It just wasn't a subject that anyone mentioned. It was a bit spooky really.

Then, just after my eleventh birthday, the one where I got that handbag, they woke me – the strange sounds of raised voices, the movement of furniture, things being smashed. I lay there for a while hoping they would go away. But they didn't.

I was scared. So I got up and opened the door to my room. It was then that I recognised the sound. Dad. He was shouting – screaming almost. I couldn't understand it. It didn't really sound like him. Not the dad I knew. Not the one who would play with me or take me to the park. Who was this strange man who was in my dad's body, and using his voice? Why was he shouting? And then there was Mum. Why did she sound so terrified?

I couldn't move for a minute. I just stood there, frozen to the spot. Until gradually I made myself kneel down at the top of the stairs and peer through the banister rails. I looked at Dad. He wasn't just shouting. He was stumbling. He was falling all over the place. He could hardly stand up, let alone walk.

Slowly, gradually, it dawned on me. He was drunk. Absolutely blind drunk.

I guess I grew up a lot that night. Before, I knew that Dad enjoyed drinking. Every night, after coming in from work, he'd have a glass of something. But he didn't drink very much. Well, we never saw it, anyway. We didn't know what happened after we went to bed. How could we? We didn't see it or hear it.

But I did that night. And every other night. That was why, from then on, I found it so difficult to get to sleep. Most nights I would lie there and wait for it to start. Then, when it did, I would check on my brother and sister (I wanted to be sure that they were alright) and then creep out to sit at the top of the stairs.

I spent many nights behind those banisters, looking at my dad, and crying. Those are some of my strongest childhood memories. The empty bottles on the floor. The broken glasses. Dad stumbling about and shouting, always shouting.

Why did he have to drink so much? Why couldn't he stop? Couldn't he see what it was doing to our house, and to Mum? Didn't he know what she might do – again? Didn't he care?

2

*What is a cynic? A man who knows the price of everything
and the value of nothing.*

Oscar Wilde (*Lady Windermere's Fan*, 1892)

Not all treasure is gold and silver, mate.

Jack Sparrow, *Pirates of the Caribbean*
(Walt Disney Pictures, 2003)

'One pound fifty pence.'

'No.'

'OK then, one pound.'

'No.'

'Well, what then?'

'Nothing. I'm not paying you a penny. You should do it
because you live here. How much do we do for you, for
goodness sake? Do I charge you for the food I cook or the
clothes I wash? Do I give you a bill for cleaning your room
or driving you to a party? And now you won't even cut
the lawn without some money.'

'Oh, don't go on about it, Mum. Don't nag. I'm sorry. All
I said was that I wanted to earn some cash – and I thought
this was a good way of doing it. You want the grass cut. I
want some money. I just thought we could do a deal.'

'Money, money, money. That's all you think about.'

'It's not all I . . . Well, perhaps . . . Look, you've got to have money. Of course you have. You can't do anything without it.'

Andy's mum smiled and poured him another mug of tea.

'You wait. In a couple of years' time I'll have cars, houses, anything I want.'

'You reckon?'

'Yeah, by the time I'm twenty I'm gonna be a millionaire.'

'Blimey,' said his dad, without looking up from the paper. 'That'll be one heck of a paper round.'

'You don't take me seriously, neither of you do. You just don't understand, do you?' Andy banged his fist on the table. The tea spilled over the edge of his mug. 'I mean it, I'm gonna make a million – and I don't care who I tread on as I do it.'

'Does that include us?' asked his mum.

Andy stopped for a second. Of course it didn't include them. He loved his mum, even though she did seem to nag him a lot at the moment. And his dad. He didn't like the way his dad poked fun at him. But, well, that was Dad – and he loved him. He loved his home too. Sure, they argued – and, if he was honest, he would have to admit that it was usually him who started it. But it was a great place to be, at home with his mum and dad, around the kitchen table with Mum's seemingly endless supply of tea. Did it include them? Of course not.

He looked his mum straight in the face. 'Of course it includes you,' he said. 'Look, life is what you make it. And I'm not gonna let anyone hold me back, especially not you two. You don't understand. You don't really care about me. I'm not staying around here. First chance I get – I'm off. I'm going.' Andy stormed out.

His mum and dad sat in silence as they mentally counted the stamping sound on the stairs. They paused a second for him to walk around the landing, and waited to wince at the noise that the bedroom door would make when he slammed it. When it happened, as it always did, they half-smiled at each other but didn't speak, because they knew that the ritual was not yet quite complete – until the music had started at full volume. It never took long. And, strangely, it always seemed to be a bit of a relief to them. The thump-thump noise of his latest purchase vibrating through the ceilings and walls meant that the show was over. It was complete. And it wouldn't be too long before Andy came back downstairs again – as if nothing had ever happened.

They had seen it and heard it many times before. How often had he said that he had had enough of them? How many times had he warned them that he was going to leave home and live his own life? He never did it of course. It was all talk. Except that this time it wasn't.

* * *

Living on the estate wasn't easy for any of the families. But for Sharon it was particularly difficult.

You see, a lot of the estate was in darkness. The kids used the lights as targets for their catapults. Most nights a gang of them would collect bits of stone from the derelict houses behind the pub, and then pick on one bulb to attack. It took quite a lot of hits to put it out. But that was the challenge. In between the cigarette breaks and the trips to the chip shop they would work away at it. The one who eventually made it go dark always got the biggest cheer. He was the star. He had put another area of the estate into darkness.

The darkness scared Sharon. Of course she tried not to let her fear show in front of others. She couldn't. Fear wasn't allowed. You had to be hard. 'I'm well 'ard' – that was what she said. It was what everyone said on her estate. That was what everyone wanted to be, anyway.

Sharon had every reason to be scared of the dark. Well, not of the dark itself, of what happened in the darkness. But the mind makes links and associations, so fear travels. She couldn't quite remember when this journey started. Perhaps it was when she was eight or nine. Maybe even earlier. Those distant memories were as uncertain and mysterious as they were powerful and terrifying.

What she could remember clearly was how regular it had become in her teenage years. Each night she would try to get to sleep as quickly as she could. Hoping that, somehow, sleep would protect her from the horrors of the darkness. She even tried pretending that she was asleep. She had practised how to lie perfectly still and breathe in a steady, slightly snuffly way. It didn't stop it, of course. But somehow, it did seem to make it easier for her. Perhaps she could pretend that it hadn't really happened – that it was just a dream, a terrible nightmare.

But it is not easy to get to sleep when you are waiting for a sound. A noise that, itself, has become linked with fear – and is part of the road along which it travels.

Strangely enough, it was actually the quietness she heard – the lack of sound. It was the almost silent footsteps on the stairs – given away only by the one that creaked near the top. Then the loose floorboard on the landing. That made a slightly different sound. It was deeper than the creaky stair. More like a groan really. That particular noise always made every muscle in her body tense as she waited for the slow turning of the handle, then the scrape of the door against that bit of lino that had been worn out and bent back by too many feet coming through her doorway at night. Each time bringing pain and confusion – and pushing the fear further along its path.

It stopped for a while when Aunt Sarah came to stay. Night after night Sharon waited for the familiar sounds but they never happened. Each morning she awoke, wondering if perhaps she'd managed to get to sleep before he came. She thought perhaps she had slept through it all. But she couldn't believe that. She knew how it felt in the morning. And now it didn't feel like that at all. It was over. It was gone. Perhaps she could erase it from her memory. Maybe she could believe that it had all been one big dark dream – and now she had woken up into a bright, light, new day.

She wanted to hug her Aunt Sarah, to hold on to her and never let her go. She couldn't understand how Aunt Sarah had turned on the light. Perhaps she had caught him on the stairs. Perhaps he just couldn't do it when his sister was in the house. She didn't know, but she didn't really care either. Whatever it was, it was all over now. The light was on. And it was on to stay – because Aunt Sarah was here.

Sharon liked having her around. And she seemed to like her. She bought her presents. They were only silly little things, but they meant a lot to Sharon. And they would sit and talk together or watch TV. Often the others would go out in the evening and they would ask Aunt Sarah to go with them. But she used to make some excuse about waiting for a phone call or having to wash her hair. Really she just wanted to stay in so that they could be together. When she said those things she would look at Sharon. And she was happy to go along with it. It wouldn't be kind to say that there never was any phone call and that she never did wash her hair. This was their little secret. It was their way of having some time together.

Aunt Sarah wasn't like the others. She didn't sit in an armchair on her own as they watched TV. She sat on the settee right next to her. They cuddled up close to each other. Aunt Sarah even put her arm around Sharon. She liked that.

It was nice when she stroked her hair. And her face. And down her arms. And around her waist. And down her legs. And up again.

Sharon couldn't believe it. Not her Aunt Sarah. No.

She felt her muscles tense. She felt her stomach turn.

And outside, in the street, the kids cheered as they put out another light.

*   *   *

Andy thought that this would be a moment that he would never forget. It seemed that he had been waiting for it for a lifetime. How many times had he lain in bed and imagined what it would feel like? Sometimes he had heard others talk about it. 'You never forget your first,' they'd say. And he hoped they were right.

Now, here he was, standing in the queue, waiting with such anticipation.

He'd slogged hard all week. If he was honest, work wasn't quite what he had thought it would be. Well, he didn't really know what he had expected. All he knew was that it must be better than living at home and going to school. Whatever it was like it would be better than that. And it was. He thought perhaps he was happier than he had ever been.

He particularly liked the clear, clean sense of anticipation at the beginning of the day. He made sure that he arrived early each morning just so that he could stand there in the post-room, on his own. There was something about the quiet emptiness of the room first thing in the morning that gave him a feeling of purpose and meaning. He wasn't quite sure what it was – and he didn't want to think too deeply into it. But he loved the sense that he was at last part of the great British economy. Sure he was just a very small cog in a very big wheel. But it was a start.

Mark and Joe seemed to appreciate his efforts. They worked together in a team receiving the mail and sorting it – first into departments, then into offices and then into individuals. Mark had shown Andy what to do when he first arrived. It couldn't really be called training because it was so haphazard. But at least Andy had picked up the general idea and both Mark and Joe were always there to answer his questions when he got stuck. They never seemed to mind when he put envelopes in the wrong place, or didn't know where the larger packages should go. In fact Mark and Joe didn't seem to mind about anything much – except the football scores.

Neither of them played the game. Not seriously anyway. But they watched it whenever it was on the TV and they went to as many matches as they could. Like most football fans they had very strong opinions and would take any opportunity to share them. Given half a chance they could spend hours talking about matches that had taken place years ago, and which they still seemed to remember in great detail. Sometimes they would carry on sorting the post as they reminisced with one another. But mostly they would just stand there, with envelopes and packages hanging loosely from their fingers as they talked about the finer points of a penalty decision or an off-side ruling.

Andy couldn't talk while he sorted. It took all his concentration. Because he didn't just try to put the envelopes in the right trays. He wanted to learn the names and the departments. By the end of the first day he not only knew the proper titles for each different division, but also which floor they were on and whether they were covered by the special security arrangements which Mark and Joe had said they were supposed to observe – but had also told him not to worry too much about anyway.

Over the next couple of days he set about learning as many staff names as he could. Some of them were easy because they had lots of post, but others he only came across occasionally. Still, as long as he concentrated and tried not to be put off by the incessant chatter about transfer fees and injuries, he could make progress. By the Thursday he had most of the regular names pretty clear in his mind. He knew the difference between Mr Guest who worked in accounts on the fourth floor and Mr Guest who handled contracts on the seventh. He even had a fairly clear picture of the various offices where all of the different Mr Smiths worked.

Mark and Joe were pleased with their young trainee. They didn't really know how he did it. Nor did they care. They were just happy to see that he sorted so much post so quickly. They made sure that he got the biggest bags when they came in. And when he was at the other end of the table they quietly put some of their pile on top of his as well. This gave them more time to spend with the really important work of the day – discussing who the manager should pick for the new England team.

Sometimes they did find Andy's earnestness a bit too much. 'Hey, loosen up will you mate?' they would say. But they didn't ever get cross with him – not just because his keenness reduced their work-load, but also because Andy did loosen up – each night after work in the Red Lion. Sure, he was sometimes a bit annoying when he tried to ask them whether they were certain that they had properly sorted that last bag of envelopes that had been delivered just before the end of the day – as if they knew or cared. But they really liked being with him. After a pint or so of lager he did begin to relax – and he always had a funny comment or story that made them laugh.

It was good to laugh, and to laugh out loud, because it made the girls put down their glasses of port and lemon and glance over in their direction. And they often did look, when Andy was with them. He was a good-looking lad – tall, quite muscular for his age, and with the boyish freshness that some girls really seem to like. Yes, Mark and Joe were very pleased with Andy.

Andy's mum and dad were not so happy. They couldn't hide their disappointment when he gave up on his schooling. They were glad that he had got himself some qualifications, but they knew that he could have gone much higher. On to college certainly, possibly even university. Who knows. But Andy thought he knew. He knew how he was going to get on in life and nothing was going to stand in his way.

Well, he certainly hadn't hung around. Just a few weeks after walking out of the school gates for the last time he had walked into the job at Thurman and Sloane. Sure he was only in the post-room at the minute but at least it was a start. He wouldn't be sorting packages and delivering letters for long. Soon he would be sorting deals and delivering ultimatums. This was the city of London, the centre of the financial world, after all.

'It's just a start. You wait and see.'

'Yes dear,' said his mum as she opened one of his suitcases and tried to work out where she could hang the clothes she had so carefully ironed and packed for him. She looked around the tiny, dark, dusty room and tried not to ask him again why he couldn't still live at home.

'Honestly, it is just a start,' he said, for at least the fifth time that evening. 'You don't think I'm going to be here for ever? I'll soon have my own flat, or a house. Then I'll rent out rooms to other people. I reckon you could get five in a house like this. Easy. Six if you divided that front room. That's possible. You could build a wall across from the fireplace to the other side in between the two windows. They'd be a bit of an odd shape but it would work. Then, if you charged each person a rent of say . . .'

His mum wasn't listening. She was looking for somewhere to put his socks.

He didn't mind standing in the queue. He quite enjoyed it, in fact. He didn't stamp around like Mark and Joe, making cutting comments about the inefficiency of the place. He'd looked forward to this all week, and nothing was going to spoil the moment. This was his first wage packet. He'd done his first week's work. And he had earned it all. When they eventually got to the front Mark and Joe just picked up their money and ran.

Andy couldn't move that fast. It wasn't just that he didn't know where to sign on the form the girl held out to him. The fact was that he didn't want to move quickly. He wanted to savour the moment. *You'll never forget your first*, he thought.

He took the little brown envelope and held it carefully between his fingers as he walked over to the side of the room. He let others push past him, as they headed for the door. But he carefully made his way to the low bench that ran down the side. He didn't sit down. He just leant against it as he gently pulled open the flap. It clearly hadn't been stuck down for long, as it came up almost complete, with only just a little bit of tearing around the edges. Andy held the flap in his right hand while he used the thumb and forefinger of his left lightly to squeeze the edges of the packet towards one another. The flap flipped back straight and the top opened to reveal a small wad of neatly folded banknotes.

Now using the thumb and forefinger of his right hand Andy carefully pulled out the notes and held them still. With one movement of his left hand he closed the flap on the odd coins that had been left behind and tucked the envelope in his jacket pocket. Now he concentrated all his attention on the wad of notes he held in his right hand.

He smiled and breathed in deeply as he began to count them very carefully. He didn't doubt that they had given him the right number. He wasn't really counting them to check the amount. He just wanted to feel them in his hand. In both hands. He passed them, one by one, from right to left – and then left to right. He ran his fingers along the full length of the top note, and then his thumb across the ends, gently flicking them like a pack of cards.

He was just about to count them again when Mark grabbed his shoulder from behind. 'Come on, mate. What are you doing?' he said, with more impatience in his voice than Andy had heard all week. 'We're not hanging around here all night. We've got a lot of lager to get through. Joe's getting the first round in already. Come on.'

'Yeah, sure,' said Andy, trying not to let Mark see how he was carefully folding the notes with his hand and putting them in his trouser pocket.

'Ready to loosen up?' said Mark.

'You bet,' replied Andy.

He'd already drunk a lot of lager that week. More than he had in the previous month when he had been living at home. Mark and Joe seemed to drink a lot. And they always wanted Andy with them. That wasn't terribly easy during the week, because he didn't have much money. He did have the cash that he had saved while he was at school. But it wasn't much. And he had to use a lot of it to pay the rent on his room and buy his food. However, tonight was different. He had a pocket full of money and he wanted a belly full of beer.

Andy really liked the feeling that swept over him after the first few pints of lager. He enjoyed the warm glow and the sense of detachment from reality. He liked the way that it made his stories seem to flow more smoothly; and his jokes seem more funny. But most of all he enjoyed the way in which it seemed to make the girls easier to talk to. He'd seen them several times in the pub that week. Mark said that they worked on the switchboard in the offices round the corner. 'They can flick my switches any time they want,' Joe said whenever they looked over – as if the more times he told it the funnier it would become.

And now tonight they were sat together around a small wobbly table from which lager was steadily dripping on to the floor. The girls didn't want to talk about their work, or about football for that matter. But they did want to listen to Andy's jokes. In fact they were a great audience. They would laugh at almost anything. And the blonde one particularly seemed to like him. She had made sure that she sat next to him when they came over. And now she was squashing up so close that almost the full length of her body was pressed against his. Andy would have been embarrassed and would have felt tongue-tied at any other time. But not after a few pints of lager. Right now he felt invincible. The best he had ever known. Here he was, away from home, with money in his pocket, beer in his stomach, mates around the table and a girl cuddling up next to him.

He didn't notice who suggested it. Nor did he remember agreeing to leave the lager that he still hadn't finished. But suddenly they were all outside the pub, in the gathering darkness, piling into Joe's rusty old van – and on their way to an Indian restaurant. Andy wasn't sure if he liked Indian food. But he liked the feeling of being with his mates and he especially liked the way the blonde girl squashed herself into the van on his lap.

Joe wanted to show them all a particular Indian restaurant on the other side of town. 'You'll love it,' he said. 'Best one in London – trust me, I know what I'm talking about.' Joe also wanted to show them all the short-cuts around the back streets – and how fast he could drive. By the time they arrived Andy was not feeling so good.

'You alright, mate?' said Mark.

'Yeah, I'm fine,' replied Andy. 'Just need a minute on my own. You go on in.'

'I'll order for you. Trust me. Look, here's the van keys. Make sure you lock it up when you come in.' Joe tossed the keys into Andy's lap and led the way along the pavement.

Andy sat quietly and closed his eyes. But that didn't help. It just seemed to make everything spin even faster. He rubbed his face and shook his head. But nothing made him feel any better. He felt both hot and cold as he got out of the van. He walked up the pavement and into the end of an alleyway where he leant against a shop wall and waited for the inevitable. He was glad that it was dark and there was no-one around to see or hear him spread his lager down the side of the shop. It took three or four attempts until he was completely empty and his stomach had stopped heaving.

When it was all over he straightened himself up, wiped his mouth on his sleeve and walked back towards the van. He felt much better now. He thought that he might even fancy an Indian meal. Well, in a minute or two anyway, after he had sat in the van for a while.

'Been making a pavement pizza have we Andy?' Joe laughed as he leant against his van. 'I just wanted to check that you weren't going to do it all over my seats. Are you finished?'

'Yeah, I'm fine now. Much better. Great,' Andy replied.

'Good, 'cos someone's come out to see you while the rest of us carry on eating.'

Joe walked off towards the restaurant as Andy opened the van door and found the blonde girl sitting on the back seat. She smiled and reached out both arms to him.

'Thought you might like someone to keep you company,' she said.

When he crawled into his tiny bed in his dingy room much later that night Andy thought to himself, *They're right – you never will forget your first time.*

3

They didn't seem to have faces. Well, if they did then she couldn't see them. She couldn't really see much through the fog that covered everything. It hid the shapes and greyed out the colours. It muffled the sounds and distorted the voices. But she knew they were looking for her – again.

Almost every night they would come through the woods. It always began in the same way. She heard a twig break, then a branch scrape – and she knew it was starting again.

She tried to run away towards the park. It would be sunny there, and safe, where the other children were. There would be mums and dads pushing their kids on the swings and helping them down the slides. There would be a sand-pit to play in, and a paddling pool. There would be ice-cream in cones with a chocolate flake and strawberry sauce that ran down the side. There would be picnics with sandwiches and crisps and lemonade and biscuits – particularly those little ones with the swirl of hard coloured icing on top. She loved those. She liked to take one in her mouth and suck the sweet icing until it melted away to nothing.

But the icing was never sweet in the woods. It was all

slimy and it made her choke. And she didn't want it. Not again. She had to get away. She had to escape. She wanted to run. Desperately she tried to make her legs move. But they wouldn't. She told them to get her out of there, but they did nothing. She didn't know what was wrong with them – but whatever it was they wouldn't work. They just wouldn't. Sharon tried to shout. She tried to scream.

But nothing happened. She just lay there. And felt a small trickle of sweat run down her back.

She breathed in and out again very deeply; and waited until her heart stopped thumping against her ribs. She knew there was no point her calling for someone to come to her. No matter how much she wanted to be held and comforted she knew that would never happen. She just had to stay there, on her own, until she could get back to sleep again.

Sharon reached out and grabbed the edge of the bed covers. In one smooth movement she pulled them up and over her head. That always seemed to make her feel better. She was in her own private world under that blanket. Where she didn't have to feel afraid. She didn't have to feel pain. She didn't have to feel anything.

In 2002 there were 29,200 children judged to be at risk of abuse in the UK (figures from the Office for National Statistics).

* * *

Everything always seemed to be broken in our house. Furniture, cups, plates, doors, windows. Everything. It wasn't as if we had a lot in the first place.

When I was young Dad was working as a roofer and he didn't earn very much money at all. He had to get up early – and he'd usually left the house before we even had breakfast. I didn't realise at the time how tough it must have been for him. Well you don't, do you, when you're only a kid? All I knew was that Daddy used to climb on roofs. I wasn't really sure how he did it. But I knew it was dangerous. And cold. We were living in Bradford at the time and it can get pretty freezing up there. There's a lot of rain and snow in the winter. But Dad would go out to work whatever the weather. He told us that he had to – even if he had one of those really bad headaches he used to get some mornings. What else could he do?

Mum worked as well – as much as she could, what with three kids to look after. She had odd jobs serving in shops and packing in factories. Nothing really regular or stable, you realise, just whatever she could get.

At the time I didn't know that Dad drank too much at night. I had no idea how aggressive and violent he could become when he was drunk. All I knew was that everything seemed to be broken in our house. If ever I said anything about it Mum would fix me with one of her stares and say, 'Jacqui, just leave it.'

Sometimes Mum would come home with some new plates or cups that she had picked up somewhere or other. And we'd eat off them for a week or so. Until one morning, when we would find them in the bin – in hundreds of tiny pieces. When Dad got in a drunken rage, you see, he would sometimes be so angry that it wasn't enough just to throw an odd plate or two. He had to smash the whole lot. If they were laid out on the table he would stretch out his arm and sweep it across the surface – pushing them all on to the floor. Then he would kick the door off its hinges or put his fist through a window.

I don't know how Mum coped with it. I guess she understood some of the reasons why Dad was like this. She knew his background you see. She knew what it had done to him.

But we didn't know anything. We just knew that we didn't have very much – and we had to put up with it.

Our house didn't even have a bathroom like others did. There was a big tin bath that my parents kept in the yard. And when we all needed to get clean Mum would put it in the kitchen and fill it with water. Later, when I was at school down south, we learned a bit about social conditions in recent history – and how people didn't have bathrooms or toilets. But I couldn't admit that I had lived in a place like that just a few years before.

Actually, to be honest, I quite liked that bath. We kids would all get in together and it was fun being with one another in the kitchen – Mum's room.

We weren't so keen on the toilet though. We didn't have one in the house. When we needed to use it we had to go out of the door, up the street a bit, and in through our next door neighbour's garden. Then at the back we would find a block of three toilets. One of them was ours. Try doing that in the middle of the night when it is freezing cold and pouring with rain.

But I've got some good memories of that house. It had a huge attic that we could get into. We would play there for hours, all of us kids. We were in our own world in there. We could play mums and dads, or doctors and nurses. In fact we could play whatever we wanted. We could be whoever we wanted. It was a magical world of let's pretend which somehow detached us from the reality downstairs.

But the reality downstairs could not be avoided for ever. The fact was that Mum had had enough of it. I guess there is only so much you can take. How long can you cope with seeing things broken around you? How long can you put up with a life like she had?

I don't blame her for leaving us. Not now, anyway.

She'd put up with an awful lot for a very long time. And now she wanted a life for herself. She wanted to be able to buy things and know that they were not going to be broken the next week. She wanted to be able to earn money and save it up for something she really wanted, instead of seeing it poured away in yet another bottle of cider or beer. She wanted to be able to sit down and relax at night, or go out to the cinema, without having to suffer yet another drunken rage.

So one day she just packed her bags and left. We didn't understand it. Where was Mummy going? We didn't know anything about the south of England. When was she coming back? She wouldn't say. Dad told us that we were now on our own and that we would have to cope somehow. We told him not to worry – that Mummy would be back very soon. But he didn't seem to take any notice of that.

It was then that we began to overhear whispered conversations about 'broken homes'. We didn't know what they were talking about. And we couldn't really ask anyone. We just had to guess. So we figured that it was something to do with the smashed-up crockery and the doors that were hanging off their hinges.

* * *

Somehow Dad managed to look after us all. I don't know how he did it. But, deep down, despite his drinking, Dad had a strong character. He could cope. I guess you have to if you are to survive the life he had lived.

I don't really know how he managed it. Perhaps he cut back on his drinking. And I don't know how he managed to persuade Mum that they should get back together again. But I am glad he did.

I remember the train journey. It was long and boring. But that didn't matter, because we were going to see Mum again. We were going to be a family once more, a normal, secure, stable family.

Initially we stayed with a distant relation. That wasn't easy. But we were eventually offered a council house and we were all so excited. This was a new start – a new beginning in a new home.

But it didn't really work out like that. Dad started drinking again. Even more heavily. Things got broken most nights. And we waited for Mum and Dad to go the same way. Once again we didn't have much in the house – and what we did possess was second-hand or broken.

This made it difficult for me when I started at grammar school. Mum and Dad were really pleased that I had passed the entrance exam. It wasn't the sort of thing that people from our family did. But I had managed it. I had made it into the posh school. Of course they were pleased. But they were also worried. Because they knew what it could be like for me there. They knew what I might have to cope with.

I didn't notice it at first. But then I started to hear the whispered comments and the secret giggles. I suppose every child wants to fit in. You can't bear the idea that you might be different. You want to be accepted. I certainly did.

It was alright for the other girls. Their parents had money. They could buy them the latest clothes. All I had was what Mum could pick up from the local jumble sale. Nothing ever fitted me properly, and nothing was ever in fashion.

It's funny how some things always stick in your memory. Well for me it was those shoes. Hideous they were. At least I thought so at the time. They're probably quite fashionable now. Strange isn't it, the way someone somewhere decides what's in and what's out? Anyway, I remember Mum bringing them home from the charity shop. This was when it wasn't trendy to buy from those kinds of places. But it was all Mum could afford when Dad drank and smashed the rest of the money away.

They were basically old lady's shoes. I took one look at them, burst into tears, and ran off to my room. Just the sight of them was enough. I knew immediately the comments the other girls would make. I knew what they would say about me and my shoes and my family.

Mum tried to come into the bedroom to talk to me. And eventually I let her in. I didn't stop crying the whole time she sat on my bed and talked. Dear old Mum. Of course she was trying to help. I couldn't blame her for the fact that we didn't have any money.

I wasn't really sure that I could blame Dad either. You see it was around that time that I found out one of the reasons why Dad drank so much. His dad, my grandfather, used to drink. Every night he would be at the club with his crowd of drinking mates. They all used to show off in any way they could. Some would brag about how much they had drunk one night – and still made it home on foot. Others would demonstrate how quickly they could down a single pint – and not bring it straight back up again. But then Granddad went one better. He decided to show off how much his son could drink.

That was a great reason to boast. Not only could he hold his liquor, but so could his son. Even though he wasn't old enough to drink legally, still he could down pints as fast as anyone. So Dad would be wheeled out and set up like some prize fighter in a ring. Granddad made it quite clear to him that the family honour was at stake. Dad knew that it would bring terrible shame on them all if he didn't drink every pint that was put in front of him. So he drank, and drank, and drank. And now, many years later, he couldn't stop. Even when his daughter desperately needed a pair of shoes so that she would not feel embarrassed at school. Still he couldn't stop enough to save the money to buy them for her.

So Mum did her best. She sat on my bed and tried to find out what was wrong with them. As if there was one little thing that she could change and then they would be perfectly alright.

She asked me if the heels were too high. Of course they were. What did she think? This was a time when low heels were fashionable. And the most trendy shoes certainly didn't have great big things on them like the ones Mum had bought.

So, with that typical look of northern determination on her face, Mum strode downstairs and into the kitchen. She picked up the shoes from the floor where I had thrown them in my tears and temper. She opened the drawer by the cooker and rummaged around until she found the bread knife – it was a long serrated one as I remember it, certainly the sharpest knife we had in the house. She laid the shoes on the chopping board one by one and set about them with the blade.

I don't know why I wore them to school the next day. I knew what people would say. It was bad enough to wear shoes that were unfashionable, let alone shoes that were second-hand. So what would the other girls' reactions be to second-hand unfashionable shoes that had been hacked about with a bread knife? It was obvious. It was inevitable.

I read somewhere that sharks can smell fear. I don't know if its true. But I'll tell you what. Young girls certainly can. They didn't even have to look at my feet that morning to know that I was going to be an easy target for their criticisms and taunts. I was in no position to fight back either with my words or my fists. I was on the ropes before I even got to school. I was defeated before I walked through the gate.

I didn't really blame the other girls. I couldn't. Because, if I was honest about it, the fact was that I wanted to be like them. I wanted to be able to criticise someone for not having the newest fashion or the latest jewellery. I wanted to be able to tease and taunt some poor unfortunate. I'm not proud of that. Of course I'm not. But that was the way it was.

No matter how horrible they were to me, I wanted to be like them. I wanted what they had. I wanted to be in their families. It wasn't that I didn't love my mum and dad. But I wanted to live like them. I wanted to be in a home where Dad wouldn't get drunk each night. I wanted to live in a house where things didn't get smashed up. And, most of all, I wanted to know that the people I loved and needed most weren't going to leave me. I wanted to know that Dad would be able to help me in the night if I called for him. And I wanted to know that Mum would still be there in the morning.

Abraham Maslow was an American psychologist and philosopher. Born in 1908, he died in 1970. He is perhaps best known for his writing on the 'hierarchy of needs'. All humans have basic physical needs and our bodies must have them met. So there is some kind of internal drive that makes us seek out food, water and warmth. However, says Maslow, this internal drive does not stop there. Once our basic physiological needs have been met we continue to be driven – to meet our psychological needs. Thus our bodies crave safety and security, a sense of belonging, of self-esteem and of self-actualization.

4

I don't really know where to start. . . I don't know when it started. . . It just hurt. Every night. Yeah, for a while he did it almost every night. . .

Sharon's mother screwed up the sheet and stuffed it back in her pocket. How many times had she read it today? Fifteen? Twenty? She had lost count. But each time it made her even more angry. Her mind raged with thoughts of what would happen. She could see the police arrive. And the social workers. She could hear the family being split up, the home gone. And all because of this stupid, selfish girl.

The moment Sharon came home her mum grabbed her by the hair at the back of her head and threw her into the kitchen. For a moment they just stood there. Almost nose to nose. Like boxers trying to win the silent psychological battle that takes place before the physical fight begins.

Then, slowly, deliberately she pulled the crumpled paper from her pocket.

'Tell me, you slag. What's this?'

When Sharon saw what her mum was holding she thought she was going to be sick.

'It's mine.'

'I know it's yours – I found it in your room.'

'You had no right . . .'

'I have every right. Don't you tell me . . .'

Sharon tried to push her mum away. But she wasn't strong enough.

'Who were you writing this for?'

'No-one.'

Sharon didn't often tell the truth to her mum – but she did that time. The fact was that she didn't write it for anyone. She wasn't really sure what she was going to do with it. Perhaps she would give it to one of her teachers. Or maybe she would post it to the police station, sort of anonymously – and see if they could work it out. But she didn't. She didn't give it to anyone. She just stuffed it in the corner of her room, behind her clothes, where it wouldn't be found – unless anyone moved her clothes, which her mum did that morning.

'Don't lie to me.'

'I'm not.'

'You are. It's all lies. You're a lying selfish bitch. Why are you doing this to us? How can you say these things? After all we've done for you.'

Sharon said nothing.

'I know what you're like. I've seen you – the way you move your body around. And now you're trying to blame your dad – and your aunt. I just can't believe it. Do you want to split us up? Is that what you want? Well it will be all your fault. It is all your fault.'

'Your fault . . . Your fault . . .' How many times had Sharon heard those words inside her own head?

Of course it was her fault. She knew it. Other dads don't do what hers had done to her. It must be her fault. That's why Aunt Sarah had done it too. That must have been her fault as well.

That was why no-one wanted to know. Because it was really all her fault. And, when she had thought about telling someone about it, when she wrote that letter, she knew that this would mean that the family would be split up. She didn't need her mum to tell her that. Or the fact that this would be her fault too. Everything was her fault. And there was nothing she could do about it.

Sharon tried to grab the paper. But her mum wouldn't let go. Like dogs fighting over a rabbit they pulled and tore and screamed and yelled. Without loosening her grip on the paper her mum put her arm around Sharon's throat and squeezed. All the anger and hatred that had built up through the day was released into that headlock. Sharon felt the strength being forced out of her. Gradually she stopped struggling and let go. Her mum continued to squeeze, even jerking at her with sudden clenches of her arm muscle.

Eventually Sharon closed her eyes and pretended to be unconscious. She let herself become limp and just hang there, waiting. When her mum did let go Sharon fell to the floor. She could hear the paper being torn again and again as she lay still, waiting for it all to be over.

* * *

She didn't know how long she lay on the floor pretending to be unconscious. It was probably only a few seconds. Just long enough for her mum to tear the letter into pieces so small that she couldn't tear them any more.

But for Sharon it was as if time stood still. It seemed that the world around her was waiting for her to make a decision. Would she just lie there and do nothing. Would she curl up her legs and bend her neck down? Would she try to pull the blanket up over her head as she had so many times before? Or would she get up and do something about it?

It could only have been a few seconds, but it was long enough. When Sharon stood up she knew exactly what she had to do.

Without saying a word to her mum, she walked through the door, up the stairs, round the corner and into her room. There she emptied her school bag on to the floor and kicked the books and files away under the bed. That bag wasn't very big – but it was probably big enough. Anyway it was all that she had so it would have to do.

It only took her a few minutes to cram as many clothes and bits of make-up as she could into the bag. It took her longer to open up the small plastic money box in which she had stuffed as many notes and coins as she could over the past few months. She had even surprised herself that she had managed to save so much. But then, deep down, she knew that this time would come and she had to be ready.

Now it was here. She was hard enough. She could do it.

And she did. She put the money in her pocket, flung the bag over her shoulder, and walked down the stairs.

When her mum heard the front door being slammed she looked up. Without getting out of her chair she could see the back of Sharon's head and shoulders as she walked out the gate. She knew what was happening. She knew what Sharon had stuffed in her bag. She had expected it for a long time.

She took a drag on her cigarette, breathed it in, and blew out a long, fine, line of smoke . . .

* * *

'So what are you gonna do now?'

'Dunno.'

'Where are you gonna stay?'

'Here, I hope.'

'Here?'

'Can I? I've got nowhere else to go.'

Sue didn't know what to say. Years ago they had been really close friends. They came from a different area of town; Sue didn't live on the estate. But they had been in the same class at primary school. They had played together each lunch-time – skipping, or cat's-cradle – whatever happened to be the craze at the time. She had seemed to be such a kind and caring girl then. She was always looking after the younger children and playing games with them. And if the teacher wanted some help then Sharon was always the first out of her chair.

Sue remembered their first day together at the secondary school – when she was really scared. She had tried to hide it. And probably managed it quite well, because no-one noticed, except Sharon. Sharon could always see if someone was upset. Sue would never forget how Sharon had reached out to her under the table, and taken her hand, and given it a squeeze when no-one was looking.

They were best friends then. Before Sharon changed.

Sue reached out for Sharon's hand. She wanted to hold it and give it a squeeze. But Sharon saw it coming and pulled her hand away as fast as she could.

'No, forget it,' she said. 'Forget I ever asked. I don't need it. I'm OK.'

'But I want you to stay her. Please.'

'No, don't bother. Forget it. I'm hard. I can cope.'

'Look, Mum always used to like you. She won't mind. And I'm on my own most of the time. I'd like you to be here.'

'No, I don't need it. I'm alright.'

'But there's plenty of room here. I can move all my old dolls and things off this extra bed and you can sleep here in my room. It will be like that time we camped together in our back garden. We can lie in bed and talk.'

'No, forget it.'

For the next half-hour Sharon and Sue played a strange game of cat and mouse – a game in which the mouse had no intention of getting away. She wanted to be caught, she just couldn't admit it. Sharon desperately wanted to stay at Sue's house. She wanted for them to sleep in the same room together. She wanted to lie in bed at night and talk. She even wanted Sue to leave her dolls on the bed so that they could be there with her.

But she kept telling her that she could cope, that she was hard. Every few minutes she said that she was going to leave, but inside she desperately hoped that Sue would hold on to her and stop her from going.

Eventually they both simply got tired of the game and agreed that Sharon should stay at least for that night.

'I'll go tomorrow,' said Sharon, knowing full well that she wouldn't.

'OK. Just for tonight then,' agreed Sue, knowing quite well that it would be for much longer than that.

* * *

Sharon gradually unpacked her bag over the next couple of days. First she laid a few of her clothes on the floor next to her bed. Then she added some more. Eventually Sue cleared out some of the drawers for her, and a corner of the wardrobe.

When the bag was empty Sharon folded it up and slid it under the bed. She never once used it for school books. In fact she never went back to the school again. Instead she managed to get a job serving in a café. It didn't pay much. But it was cash in her hand each day, and it enabled her to buy cigarettes and chips each night as she hung out with the others on the estate. Sometimes Sue came out with her in the evening. But not very often. She didn't really mix very well with the other kids – and Sharon knew that.

So sometimes Sharon would stay in with Sue in the evening – they sat and watched TV together. Sometimes they washed their hair and did each other's make-up. Sharon really liked those kinds of evenings together. But she couldn't admit it, and she couldn't do it very often. Most of the time she would go out and try to look hard.

But each night Sharon let herself in with the key that Sue had given her and hoped that Sue was still awake so that they could lie there in the darkness and talk. Most nights Sharon left it too late and Sue was fast asleep when she got in. But when she was still awake they would chat for hours.

'What's the point?' said Sharon on one of those nights. 'I was gonna leave school in a few weeks anyway.'

'Well you haven't exactly been coming recently, have you?'

'There's no point. It's all a waste of time. And they can't do anything about it.'

'Aren't you at least going to stay on and take the exams?' Sue tried not to sound like she was nagging.

'There's no point. I'm not gonna pass any of them, am I? And what good are they gonna do me?'

'Yes but it's better to have some kind of qualification rather than nothing at all.' Sue cringed inside as she said it.

'Well, who said I'm gonna have nothing at all?'

'You did.'

'No I didn't, I just said I'm not taking any of their stupid exams. I'm taking another qualification.'

Sue sat up and turned the light on. 'Have you enrolled at the college then?'

'Not the Tech. What do I want physics or chemistry for? No, I'm starting a course at the Lewis School of Modelling.'

'You're joking.' Sue could feel her eyes opening wide.

'No joke. You are looking at the next catwalk queen. You should have heard what they said.'

'Go on – tell me.'

For the next hour Sharon told her friend every detail of her day. She had been bursting to tell her all about it ever since Sue got home from school. But she decided that it would seem too soft and girly if she just blurted it all out. So she tried to be ice cool, and rock hard. She went out and ate chips with her other friends for most of the evening. But she made sure that she was home before Sue was asleep that night.

*   *   *

It hadn't been easy to find the Lewis School of Modelling, even with the instructions given on the advert. Sharon had carried the piece of paper with her as she picked her way through the back streets. She had taken it out of the local paper the day before. It wasn't as if she normally read the thing – she was always throwing them away at the café, when they had been left on the table with the dirty plates and half-drunk mugs of tea. But she had occasionally flicked through and looked at the job adverts. That was when her eye was caught by the advert for the modelling course. Apparently the Lewis School of Modelling was holding auditions for girls who would like to see if they would be any good on the catwalk.

The advert said that only a few people could make it in the modelling world, that was why models were paid so much money. So they were inviting young hopefuls to come to them for a free, honest assessment. 'We are searching for a star,' it said.

At first Sharon didn't like the idea of an audition, or any kind of an assessment. But then she thought about her occasional evenings with Sue, when they dressed up and did their make-up – and posed in front of the mirror. She looked good like that, she knew that she did. So who knows? She could have star quality. She could be a model. That would show them. Anyway, what had she got to lose? No-one would know about it even if she did fail.

So she had torn out the advert and stuffed it in her pocket. And now here she was, trying to follow the instructions and find the school. Eventually she realised that she had walked past it three times already. It didn't have the big entrance that she had expected, and it didn't look like any school she had known. It was a small door, by the side of a butcher's shop, with three names printed on it – one of which was the Lewis School of Modelling.

The door was stuck so Sharon had to push hard to get it open. But, having got this far, she was determined to see it through and an old door wasn't going to stand in her way. Nor was the pile of post and circulars that littered the bottom of the stairs. She picked her way past them and followed the sign up and to the left, where she found an open doorway with the words 'Lewis School of Modelling' stencilled on it.

'We're soon moving to our new studios,' said a voice behind her. She looked round to see a stocky, middle-aged man with a gold watch and rings. He had obviously just come out of the toilet and he pushed past before inviting her into his office.

'We are having new studios built for us on the other side of town. But, meanwhile, we can't let girls miss their opportunities to start modelling – so we are running our courses here. Just temporarily, you understand.'

Sharon said nothing, so he continued. 'I see you've got our advert. We've been flooded with enquiries. Everyone wants to be a model. But not everyone has got what it takes. We turn loads of people down. Almost every young hopeful girl who comes through those doors goes away disappointed – back to their job in a shop or the chicken factory.'

Sharon's head and shoulders began to droop.

'But, you know what, I think you might be different. Look at you standing there. You've got a presence and a poise. Those are very important in modelling, you know. Most girls take ages to learn it. But you . . . you look like you might have it. You could be a natural . . .'

He moved around behind her, looking her up and down. Sharon didn't like him. She didn't like him at all. But she liked what he said and she particularly like the idea of photo-shoots on the beach at Acapulco.

'Hang on. Calm down. I'm getting too excited here. It's just that I see the potential you've got. Sorry, I haven't even introduced myself to you yet. My name is Lewis – the name that has launched a thousand stars. And I think I may have found another.'

For the next half-hour Lewis put Sharon through a series of tests. She walked across the room again and again. She stood. She sat. She posed. She laughed. She scowled. And through it all Lewis put little marks on the clip-board he held against his chest.

When it was all over he asked Sharon to sit as he looked carefully through her score. This seemed to take for ever as he calculated and recalculated. The longer it took the more certain Sharon was that she had failed – that she wasn't going to be any good as a model. She tried to summon the strength and courage that she would need to stand up and walk out with some kind of dignity. But before she could do that Lewis looked up at her and smiled.

'It's just as I thought,' he said. 'You've got what it takes. You can be a model.'

Sharon didn't know what to say. She felt a surge of excitement within her that she hadn't known for years. It reminded her of Christmas and birthdays when she was very young. It was like the time she won the primary school prize for 'the most helpful child' and it was announced in the assembly – everyone had looked at her and cheered.

Today there was no-one to look at her or cheer. Only Lewis. But he looked as happy as she felt.

'So, what happens now?' she asked.

'You start on our modelling course straight away,' he replied.

'Wow.'

'Let me tell you about it.' He leant forward in his chair. 'It's a crash course. Really intensive, over five full days. It's hard work but if you do well enough at it you will get the Diploma in Modelling. That is your passport to success. It will enable you to get work – loads of it in your case I reckon.'

'That sounds great – when do I start?'

'How about Monday morning – 9 a.m. sharp, don't be late.'

'Don't worry, I'll be there.' Sharon stood up and turned to leave.

'Oh, well there is just one more thing,' said Lewis.

'What's that?'

'The matter of the fee for the course. It's not free, you

realise. This isn't the local comprehensive – it's a private school. You have to pay.'

Sharon's head dropped on to her chest. She hadn't thought about that. She had some money of course. Not a lot. But she had saved some of the money she had earned at the café, and added it to the money she had taken with her on the night she left home.

However, that wasn't enough to pay Lewis's fee. No way. And that was when he gave her the biggest surprise of all. He said that she had so much star quality that he would give her the course at a discount. She couldn't believe it. Was she really that good? Apparently she was.

She didn't know how to say thank you. But Lewis told her not to worry. He just gave her an enrolment form to sign and took her deposit. 'Bring the rest in when you come to start the course next Monday,' he said.

It was only when she got home and counted the cash she had that she wondered if there was any way she would be able to get enough money to pay the rest of the fee. But then she sat down and made some calculations. If the café would give her enough work, and she didn't spend anything on food or cigarettes, she reckoned she could just do it. It would take everything she had. But that was OK.

She still couldn't really believe it as she retold her story that night. And nor could Sue. It seemed too good to be true.

For what seemed like hours Sharon and Sue sat together and talked about Sharon's future life as a model. They dreamed of sunny beaches and drooling photographers, of expensive clothes and fast cars.

When Sharon eventually lay down to go to sleep, she didn't pull the blanket over her head as she normally did. That night she didn't want to hide. She wanted to breathe

the clean fresh air. She wanted to taste it, and she wanted to feel it.

In the lab I make cosmetics, in the store I sell dreams.
Charles Revlon, founder of Revlon Cosmetics

Money can be a wicked thing. It can turn men's hearts black – good men's hearts.

Edward Walker, *The Village*
(Touchstone Pictures, 2004)

5

'Hey! Don't you talk to us any more?'

Andy picked up the pile of letters that had been thrown on his desk and looked round. 'I'm sorry. I was just trying to finish this calculation. Hey, Mark, how are you guys doing?'

'Great, we're doing fine. How about you. What's life like on the second floor?'

'It's OK. I think. I haven't been here long, you know.'

'Long enough to stop going down the Red Lion.'

'Yeah, I'm sorry about that. It's just that we always go to the wine bar round the corner.'

'We – who's we?'

'Most of us from the office here – well all the clerks and secretaries anyway.'

'Oh I see,' said Mark. 'Well, it's not the same without you. Why don't you drop in some time?'

'If I get a moment I'll see if I can.'

'Cathy keeps asking where you are.'

'Cathy, who's Cathy?' Andy tried to think who Mark meant.

'You know – the blonde girl.'

'Oh,' said Andy, 'is that her name. Really? Funny, I thought she would be a Sharon or a Tracy – not a Cathy.'

'Well, that's her name anyway. She often talks about you. She wonders if she scared you off that night when we . . .'

'No,' Andy jumped in very quickly. 'Nothing like that. It's just that I have been so busy with this new job. We often have to work late. And then, when we do go out we tend to go . . .'

'To the wine bar – I know, you told me. So what is this job then?'

Andy tried to explain. But it wasn't easy, because he wasn't sure he understood it terribly well himself if he was honest. It was only a junior job as a clerk. But it meant working with lots of figures. Checking them against tables and ensuring that everything added up correctly.

He had been doing it for almost three months now and he was clearly getting better at it. But he still had a lot to learn. And of course he always made much more work for himself because he didn't just want to look up the figures, nor simply check them. He wanted to understand them. He wanted to see where the figures came from and how they were calculated in the first place. Why was it that certain projects were reckoned to be a higher risk than others? Who had worked all of this out – and how? The more he looked at it the more complicated he found the whole insurance business to be. But he wanted to understand it. He didn't want to stay as a clerk any longer than he had to. He had ambitions.

The personnel department had spotted that very soon after he arrived. That's why they only left him for a week in the post-room. They could tell he was in the wrong job there. Whoever had interviewed him had not done a terribly good job. Of course he needed to start on the bottom rung – but it should at least be on the right ladder. He should be working with paper, not delivering it. He should be writing letters, not posting them.

Andy had jumped at the chance when they offered it to him that Monday morning. He'd enjoyed his week with Mark and Joe. But it was time to move on. He was ready to leave them behind. He didn't even go down to say goodbye. He went straight back to his room to change into a suit before finding his desk over in the corner by the window amongst the other clerks on the second floor.

From there he never saw the post arrive or leave the department. And he rarely looked up from his sheets of figures when people came and left anyway. It was only when they moved the desks around and he found himself near the door that he met Mark again.

'How's Joe?' he asked

'Doing OK. His van's just packed up, you know.'

'I'm surprised it lasted that long.'

'He's having to catch the bus in now. Mind you, he tells me he often sees you on your bike.'

'Yeah. I cycle most mornings. But I won't do for long. I'm selling my bike tonight. I've put it in the paper. I'm getting a car.'

'Really – what type?'

'A Ford Capri. It's on the forecourt of the garage round the corner. Have a look. You can't miss it. It's bright yellow.'

'Pretty good for pulling, eh?'

'You got it,' said Andy.

Andy didn't get as much as he hoped for when he eventually sold his bike late that night. Some people just laughed at him and walked away. Others said that they would pay half the price he was asking. Eventually he accepted an offer and handed over the bike in return for a pocketful of notes.

The very next day, as the other clerks and secretaries

went to the wine bar after work, he headed off in the other direction – to the garage round the corner. There he handed over the wad of notes that he had carefully counted and recounted many times during the night. It wasn't as much as he had said that he would bring but the salesman said that it was enough – because the finance company would provide the rest.

He had been really surprised when he had found out how much he was able to borrow. But he wasn't going to argue. He just signed on the dotted line and drove the car away.

'I was born with nothing – so, if I die owing people money then I reckon I'm up on the deal.' Andy had heard many people say this since he had arrived in London and he reckoned that it really was a good philosophy. 'There's no point saving,' they had also said. 'By the time you've saved up for something the price will have gone up and you won't be able to afford it. Much better to buy now on credit, then pay it off out of the money you make next week, or month, or year.'

And Andy was making quite good money. Not as much as he wanted, of course. No way. But he got quite a rise when he moved from the post-room – and now he had just got another one because he had managed to get through the three-month probationary period.

He was still living in the same dingy room. But he had some new clothes. And now he had a smart car to go with them. He was pleased with himself. He was on the way up.

*   *   *

'Sorry, I'm afraid you're just too short.'

'You what?'

'You're too short, love. I can't believe they didn't tell you this.'

'But they said I was great. They said I'd get loads of fashion work. Look, I've got all the qualifications.' Sharon carefully took her diploma certificate out of her bag and held it up.

He didn't look at it. He just rolled his eyes, took a breath and said with a sigh, 'Not another one from Lewis, here we go again.'

He was a small, thin man with his hair carefully arranged over the top of his balding head in three, futile strands. A sign on the door had said 'Majestic Model Agency' but there was nothing remotely majestic about the surroundings. Just peeling paint and plastic chairs.

'Look,' he said, 'whatever Lewis told you, and I don't want to know what he told you, the fact is that you can't argue with nature. What are you – five foot four, or five?'

Sharon nodded.

'You've got to be over five nine to do fashion. They want them tall and willowy. The ironing board look, know what I mean?' He took a drag on his cigarette, rolled toothpick thin, tiny strands of tobacco dangling from the end. 'And what are your measurements? Probably 36–26–something or other?'

Sharon cringed as he looked at her as if he could see right through her clothes. This time she didn't even nod.

'Fashion models are 34–24–34. Sometimes even less than that. Look, why is it always me that has to explain this to all the young hopefuls who walk through that door? I'm sorry love, there's no way you can do fashion.'

He didn't really expect a reply, they rarely did say anything. He just watched as she tried not to cry. Usually they did. That was why he kept a box of tissues on his desk, something to give them as they went away.

But not this one. Sharon didn't cry. And that made him

look at her again. As she turned to leave, without saying a word, he watched her carefully.

Suddenly he called out, 'Hang on a second.'

'Forget it,' she said, pulling the door behind her. She wanted to slam it, but thought that would look a bit childish.

He came out from behind his desk and caught up with her at the top of the stairs. 'Hang on, I said.'

Sharon stopped and turned towards him.

'I never said you couldn't be a model, I just said you couldn't do fashion.' Sharon narrowed her eyes and looked puzzled.

'Not all models are fashion models you know.'

'So, what other kind is there?'

'Glamour, of course.'

'Glamour?'

'Yeah. Page three. Calendars. Magazines. That's the way for you. I reckon you've got what it takes.'

Sharon didn't say anything. She didn't need to. Her expression said it all.

He leaned very close. His breath smelt of peppermint. 'Listen to me, love. I'm going to tell you the truth.' He paused and smiled. 'The ones that people really love aren't the fashion models.'

'You reckon?'

'Nah. Too aloof. Too remote. You can't dream about a statue.'

'You can't?'

'No. See, what people want is someone like them. They want someone who understands. Someone they can identify with.' He waved his hand and a thin sliver of tobacco fluttered to the floor. 'The lads out there, the men in the pubs, in the garages, the factory workers, the blokes in the locker room, they love the real girls. Flesh and

blood. Curves in all the right places. The girl next door.'
He leant close again. 'You've got what they're looking for.
Trust me. I know. Glamour is the way for you. You'll be a
natural.'

'But doesn't that mean . . .'

'What?'

'Well, you know, taking my clothes off.'

He stood back and used the slightly puzzled expression
that had worked so many times before. 'I thought you
were a professional. I thought you wanted to be a model.'

'I am. I do. But . . .'

'So what's wrong with taking your clothes off. You do it
every night, don't you? You look at yourself in the mirror,
don't you? Only this way others will look as well. And
they'll like what they see. And you'll get paid for it – loads
of money. You'll have more money than you'll know what
to do with.'

Sharon didn't look convinced. That didn't surprise him.
Most of them weren't. He turned away, as he had done so
many times before.

'Darling, it's up to you. Look, I can get you a glamour
shoot tomorrow that will pay you cash in your hand –
loads of it. Take it or leave it.' He walked back to his
office. And wasn't surprised to hear her footsteps
following his.

'What would I have to do?' she said as she stood in the
doorway.

'Just topless. That's all. Nothing else. You'll get some
really nice clothes to wear and all you've got to do is pose
and pout. Lewis taught you to do that, didn't he?'

'Yeah.'

'So that's all you have to do. It doesn't take long. It's all
over quickly. And you walk out with the money.'

Sharon didn't move. 'Just topless?' she asked.

'Yeah, that's what I said. That's not hard, is it?'

'No,' she said, 'it's not hard. I can do that.'

'Right, let me make a phone call and it will all be set.'

* * *

That night Sharon didn't get home in time to talk with Sue. She stayed out late. Much later than she ever had before.

She didn't hang around for long with the others on the street either. Once she had eaten some chips and smoked a couple of cigarettes she took off on her own and walked into town.

She had no idea how many miles she walked that night, or how long she was out for. She didn't really think about where she was or what time it was. She was too intent on thinking about the decision she had taken. Or had she taken it? Was it her decision? Was that what she wanted to do? She didn't know.

She could always not turn up. She didn't have to go. It was up to her. He couldn't force her. No-one could. It was her life. She didn't have to do what others said. She could do whatever she wanted. If only she could believe what she was saying. The fact was that she couldn't really remember a time when she had felt in control of her life. There always seemed to be some invisible black pressure bearing down on her – preventing her from being free.

Sharon travelled miles that night. She stopped once to buy some cigarettes from the all-night garage. But that was all. The rest of the time she just walked, and thought, and walked and thought.

When she eventually got into bed she had made her decision. It was up to her, no-one was going to force her to do anything she didn't want to do. It was her life. It was her body.

Man is born free, and he is everywhere in chains.
Jean-Jacques Rousseau (*Social Contract*, 1762)

Sometimes, to do what's right, we have to be steady and give up the things we want most, even our dreams.
Aunt May, *Spider-Man 2* (Columbia Pictures, 2004)

'Come on in.' The door didn't move. 'It's open. Just come on in.'

But Sharon couldn't 'just' do anything. She wasn't sure if she wanted to go in or run away. Last night she had so much confidence and certainty in the power she had to make her own decisions. Last night she knew what she would do. But today she wasn't so sure. She had spent most of the morning changing her mind over and over again. Even as she walked to the studio she had doubled back on herself several times. Once she walked half-way to the café thinking that she would ask for her old job back. But then she had weighed up in her mind the difference between being a waitress or a model. And she turned round again towards the studio.

Now she was late, but she was there, stood on the doorstep, with this man's voice telling her to 'just come on in.'

Sharon took a deep breath, clenched her teeth, and pushed on the door. 'I can do this. I can cope. I'm hard enough.' She must have said those words to herself a hundred times already that day. Now she went over them again in her mind as she opened the door and walked in.

'Hello,' she called out as she slowly made her way across the carpet.

'So you're Sharon, are you?' came a reply from behind some kind of big white umbrella which had a light where the handle should be.

If Only

'Yeah, that's me.'

Sharon guessed that this must be the photographer, there didn't seem to be anyone else in the small studio. She tried to make out what he looked like, but he was hidden behind the umbrella thing.

'I wasn't sure if you were going to turn up. I thought you'd be another no-show. This is your first time, isn't it.'

'Yeah, suppose it is, what about it?'

'Oh nothing, don't worry, you'll be fine. Anyway I'm here to look after you.'

The photographer appeared from behind the light reflector and Sharon got her first look at him. He wasn't at all how she imagined he would be. He didn't look seedy. He didn't have the greasy hair and leering eyes that she had expected. He didn't look at all like the picture she had seen in her mind throughout the morning, and the night before.

Wow, she said to herself under her breath, *I could quite fancy him.*

'Sorry, I haven't introduced myself. My name's James, I'm your photographer this afternoon.' He smiled at her. It was the kind of smile that she hadn't seen for a long time – warm and friendly and inviting.

He's too old for me, but I could still fancy him, Sharon thought to herself.

'As I said, don't worry. I'll look after you. There's nothing to it really. Just a few glamorous photos of you looking beautiful. That won't be difficult will it?'

'No, I suppose . . .'

'Great,' he said, interrupting her. 'Now we haven't got long. The first thing is to get you used to the camera. You've never done any photographic work before, have you?'

'No,' she said, 'I haven't. But I did a modelling course. I know how to stand and move and things.'

'OK then,' James said, 'let's start with that.' He switched on a tape player and a familiar tune filled the air.

'Come over here and we'll see how you move about for the camera. Now, what are you wearing under that?'

Sharon didn't move.

'What is it? Just jeans and T-shirt. That's fine. Slip your coat off and throw it over there. Then go on to that raised area over here.'

Sharon did as he said, but she still wasn't sure whether she wanted to. As she picked her way past the lights and stepped up on to the small stage she could feel every muscle in her body gradually become tense. Her stomach seemed to collapse inside her and she wondered if she was going to be sick. For a moment she thought of running out of the door and back to the café. But she said to herself again, 'I can do this. I can cope. I'm hard enough.'

Sharon moved to the centre of the stage, stood still and breathed deeply.

'OK, in your own time,' said James. 'Just walk around and do some poses. Imagine you're on the catwalk in Milan or Paris.'

Sharon tried to loosen up the muscles in her arms and her legs. She tried to ignore the feeling in her stomach. James smiled at her and nodded. She ignored him and concentrated on the beat of the music. Eventually she put her hands on her hips and leant her head forward towards the camera.

'Great!' said James as the shutter clicked several times. He smiled and blew her a kiss.

She pouted her lips and blew him one back.

'Great. Super. Excellent,' James exclaimed as the camera gave out a series of clicks in rapid succession. 'Now move about.'

So Sharon did. She moved and posed and strutted and posed again.

And all the time James said, 'Great. Super. Excellent.' And clicked his shutter. 'Now crouch down . . . Look towards me . . . And pout . . . Great. Super. Excellent. Now lean against that couch . . . and drape yourself across it . . . and look up at me . . . ooh, blow me another kiss . . . I love it when you do that . . . Great. Super. Excellent.'

And so it went on. The shutter clicked almost continually without James stopping for a moment. Sharon lost track of time. And she lost the tension that had been binding up her body and mind. She began to feel a sense of freedom and liberty. This was her body, and she was doing with it whatever she wanted to do. She had chosen to come here. She had decided to do glamour modelling. And now here she was, doing it, and doing it well.

'Great. Super. Excellent,' continued James.

And there was something else. What was it? Some feeling with which she wasn't really familiar. Something that she hadn't known much in her life at all. Something that seemed to belong to other people and not her. What was it?

Power, that was it. Power. She felt powerful. She was in control. She was calling the shots. When she moved in a particular way James responded with one of his 'Great. Super. Excellent' expressions. He was reacting to her. She could manipulate him. She was powerful. She was in control. She loved it.

'Phew,' said James, suddenly. 'You were great. Wow, I'm worn out. Look, I need to take a break.'

Sharon stood up straight and looked down at him. She didn't need to stop. She didn't want to stop. She was enjoying this. But if he really needed it, then OK, let's give him a break for a while.

As she stepped down off the little stage James came to her and gave her a gentle kiss on the cheek. 'I can't believe you've never done photographic work before. That was brilliant. You were gorgeous. Now let's find some beautiful clothes to match you. Come over here.'

James led Sharon over to the corner of the studio, where two racks of clothes stood against the walls. He took her gently by the shoulders and stood her in the middle. Then he turned round and began to work his way through the hangers. 'No, that's too old-fashioned. No, that's too big . . .'

Occasionally he took out something and gave it to Sharon to hold up against herself while he moved a step back to get a full view. This felt so strange to Sharon. She had never picked out clothes with a man before. It wasn't something her dad had ever done with her. She had dreamed about it sometimes though. Not about shopping with her dad, of course, but with some boyfriend. Not like the ones that she had hung out with on the estate. But some guy who would take her to glamorous boutiques that were tucked away down back streets, and spend all his money on buying some outrageously expensive little black number.

It was all just a dream of course, a fantasy. That sort of thing didn't happen to girls like her. But she had enjoyed it. As she was enjoying the attention that James was giving her now. She liked many of the clothes that he pulled out for her. She wanted to try them on. In fact she was a bit disappointed when he frowned and said, 'No, that's not good enough.' But she knew that he was trying to find exactly the right one for her.

Eventually he exclaimed, 'Now, this is it. This is perfect.'

He pulled out a long, flowing, jet-black dress. It was silky and smooth. And it had gold fastenings down the front.

'Hey, look, we've got several of these so there's bound to be one that fits you perfectly. Do you like it?' he asked.

'You bet,' replied Sharon. 'Can I try it on?'

'Of course you can. It'll look great on you. It's very slinky, so don't wear anything underneath, will you?' James said with a smile. 'Did they tell you to bring your own make-up?'

'Yeah, I've got it here.'

'Great. You'll need quite strong colours because of the lights. I expect they told you that as well, didn't they? Anyway, if you have a problem just give me a shout. I'll go over there and set up the cameras and open a bottle of wine while you get ready.'

'Great, super, excellent,' said Sharon with a wink and a smile.

She looked for somewhere to change, but there wasn't anywhere. She turned round and could see that James wasn't looking in her direction, he was too busy adjusting the lights and moving the stage set around. So she moved as quickly as she could to take off her clothes and replace them with the dress. Her make-up took a bit longer because she wanted to get it exactly right. For a moment she wished that Sue was there with her. She thought back to the evenings when they would make each other up and do their hair. But then she smiled to herself as she realised that she couldn't tell Sue what she was going to do in this studio. Sue wouldn't be able to cope with that. But then Sue couldn't cope with most of her life. Sure they were friends when they were younger, but not now. It was time to grow up. It was time to move on.

'As soon as I've got my money from this modelling I'll move out. I'll get a flat of my own. Maybe buy a house. And a car. Or a yacht,' Sharon dreamed to herself as she applied the finishing touches to her lips.

'There. That's it' she said as she blew herself a kiss in the mirror. 'I'm irresistible.'

Sharon didn't talk at all to Sue that night.

She spent the evening out on her own walking around town. She wasn't quite sure what to do with herself. She didn't want to hang out with the kids on the estate. They were just too young and immature. When she was a kid herself she had been happy to sit around with them throwing stones and eating chips. But not now. She had grown up. She was a model. She was 'great, super, excellent'. Those words continually echoed around her head.

Actually she wanted to go to the Rising Sun. That was the pub where all the older ones hung out. A lot of them had motorbikes and they were all parked in a row outside, with their gleaming chrome and huge handlebars. She had often stood and looked at them, longing for the time when she would be old enough to go in and be a part of that gang. But she had always been too young and had to go back to hanging around the chip-shop with the other kids.

Now she wasn't. Now she was old enough. She was a model. She was earning big money. Or at least she would be when she got paid. That was why she couldn't make her entrance into the pub that night – she didn't have any money. She hadn't had any money for quite a while now. She thought she would be paid for the modelling she did that day. That was what the agency had told her. But James explained that he needed a lot more photos and he could only pay her once she had given him the ones he needed. So she had to go back again the next day.

She was quite happy to do that, of course, who wouldn't be? Another opportunity to do all that again with James. To have all those experiences, those pleasures. She couldn't wait. Tomorrow couldn't come fast enough as far as she was concerned.

But now it was night-time and she was back in the room with Sue, who was fast asleep. Should she wake her up? Should she tell her what had happened? No. She couldn't.

She couldn't tell her what it felt like to have so much power over James. She couldn't say how she had posed and pouted. She couldn't describe what it was like to hear James tell her that she was so beautiful, and so seductive. She couldn't demonstrate how she had moved around so provocatively. Nor could she describe how the gold clasps on the front of the dress seemed to keep coming undone. Or how, after a while, she had decided not to do them up again. She couldn't tell her how her body had driven James wild with passion for her. Or how, eventually, James said he couldn't resist her any more, how he had put down the camera and joined her on the stage. And she certainly couldn't tell her what she and James had done together on the couch.

6

'Hey, Andy! How are you doing, son? It's great to hear from you.'

'Fine, Dad. I'm doing great.'

'How's the job?'

'Brilliant. Couldn't be better. I've just got a pay rise.'

'What, again?'

'Yeah, again. I told you. Some more promotion. I'm doing great.'

'Well, I suppose you are.'

For a moment neither of them said anything. They weren't quite sure what to say. Then Andy's dad broke the silence.

'So, to what do we owe the great honour of a phone call? We haven't heard from you for weeks.'

'I know, I kept on meaning to call but never seemed to get around to it. Life is so busy you know. I'm working all hours – there's always too many deadlines to meet and things to do. And then, when I'm not in the office I always seem to be out at some party or other, or in a pub or a wine bar. You know how it is, Dad.'

'I'm not really sure I do, son. It's all a bit quieter around here if you remember. My life is a hectic whirl of reading the paper and pottering in the garden – with occasional visits to work just to fill in the time.'

'Oh come on, Dad, you work very hard.'

'Yes I do. But I don't wear myself out with it. You've got to take time to sniff the roses you know, son.'

'If you say so, Dad. Anyway I am going to come home to sniff your roses if that's OK with you.'

'That's marvellous, terrific. We knew you would eventually. We knew you wouldn't really want to be up there on your own. We've kept your room exactly as it was. Same posters and . . .'

'No, Dad, don't get carried away. I'm not coming home to stay. I like it up here. I like the life. It's brilliant. I wouldn't change it for anything. What's the point of sniffing roses if you can sniff money instead? I want to come home – but only for the weekend.'

'Oh . . . I see.'

'Don't say it like that, Dad.'

'Well how do you want me to say it?'

'Look, Dad, do you want me to come home or not? I'm quite happy just to stay here you know.'

'I'm sorry. Of course we want you to come. When are you thinking of?'

'This weekend, if that's alright.'

'What, tomorrow you mean?'

'Well, the day after. I'll come down sometime late on Saturday and stay through to Sunday night – that be OK?'

'Fine, great. Your mother will be pleased.'

As soon as he had finished talking to his dad, Andy sat down to think through how he was going to arrive at his parents' house. It wasn't easy for him to decide what kind of impression he wanted to make. Whatever he did, he wanted to make an entrance. He had to impress them and the neighbours who were bound to be watching. They had to realise what a hot-shot successful businessman he was becoming.

Andy day-dreamed for a moment about jealous glances and whispered comments of 'how well he is doing in the city'. He thought of his old friends from school who were still back there in his home town. Some were still studying. Others were in dead-end jobs wrapping up things in the local shop or making holes in things in the local factory. He thought that it would be a good idea to meet up with some of them while he was there. He imagined how they would react to him.

After a few minutes Andy stopped dreaming and decided to make a few more phone calls. It took him quite a while to find the numbers which had been scribbled in an old school exercise book. Before he called each one he transferred it into his new Filofax. Each time he was glad that he had yet another entry that he could put in the pages and yet another appointment he could put in his calendar.

Deep down, I'm pretty superficial.
Ava Gardner (1922–1990)

You can conform to what other people expect or you can be yourself.
Katherine Watson, *Mona Lisa Smile*
(Columbia Pictures, 2004)

Andy's mum was the first to realise who it was that was arriving. Both she and his dad had heard the slight screech of the tyres as the car came around the corner, and then the louder sound as the driver suddenly applied the brakes and came to a halt outside their house. Then they recognised the regular, low, rhythmic thump coming from inside the car. It was the same sound that they had heard so many times, when he had stormed up to his bedroom. They looked at each other and smiled, before they stood up and opened the door.

'Well,' said his mum as she watched her son climb out of his car, 'he certainly looks smart. He's got his hair cut differently as well. And I haven't seen that shirt before.'

'Great car, son,' said his dad as he walked towards him. 'Looks even better than you described it.'

'Well, I don't want to boast, you know. But you should see what speed this thing can do. Come and have a look inside.'

They didn't really say hello. They just looked at the car. Andy showed his dad all around it, and inside, and under the bonnet. Meanwhile his mum simply stood there, on her own. She didn't know whether to join in with looking at the car, or just to wait for Andy to notice her. She decided to wait and be patient.

Eventually Andy did notice her. He felt a sharp pang of guilt that he hadn't said hello to her or anything. But, then, he always felt uncomfortable at these times and he didn't quite know what to do.

Should he go for plan A – and treat her coldly as if he was grown up now and didn't need childish affection? Or should it be plan B – where he would warmly embrace her as the prosperous son returning home after making his fortune in the big bad world. He didn't know which one to adopt. And he was a bit annoyed that he had allowed himself to become distracted with the excitement of showing off his new toy to his dad. Perhaps that hadn't really looked cool. Perhaps he had already blown his image.

So he adopted plan B. And he played the part very well. His mum responded in the way that he had hoped. And it all seemed to go according to the script.

Later that evening, when she had fed him his favourite meal, and sat listening to all his stories of the success he was having in London, Andy's mum reflected upon the changes that had taken place in her son. He hadn't been away long but he seemed so different.

She couldn't quite be sure what it was. Of course, he looked different. He had a new hairstyle and new clothes. But it wasn't that. That was superficial, it was something much deeper than that. It wasn't what he looked like, it was what he was.

He spoke differently. Was that it? He wasn't talking about his normal friends or what they had been doing together. Instead he spoke about deals and risks. He talked about contracts and indemnities. It was a language that neither of his parents understood. They tried to follow him. They tried to ask intelligent questions and to smile and nod in the right places. But really they weren't at all sure what he was going on about. Was it that which was different then? Was it his topics of conversation? Was it the things he said? No. It wasn't that. It was something else. What was it?

Andy's mum folded her arms and rested her elbows on the kitchen table. She looked at her son intently as he continued to talk about some contract or other that he was working on at the moment, and the pages of tables that he had to use for some reason or other. He thought that she was listening. He was pleased that he was impressing her so much. But actually she was neither impressed nor was she listening. She was simply trying to figure out what was so different about her son.

It was then that the penny dropped. It was then that she realised. The change was small. It was subtle. It wasn't easily noticeable. In some ways one might think that it wasn't a change at all. But it was. And it was significant, it was important.

Andy was living out his dream. And loving it. For so long he had told his parents that he was going to make a fortune, that he was going to be rich and successful. At that time it was just words. It was simply Andy talking big again. It was fantasy. It was cloud cuckoo land. They had often talked about it as they had lain in bed at night trying to go to sleep; or in the morning after their first cup of tea. 'Our son the dreamer,' they had said to each other. And that was what they thought it was – just his dreams of making it big, and being a millionaire. 'He'll grow out of it,' they had always said; 'dreams don't last.'

But now it didn't seem so much like a dream. Now it wasn't just a fantasy. Here was their son sitting at the kitchen table. And he wasn't talking of wild ideas and elaborate speculations about the things he was going to do. He was talking about his job, the work he was doing, the money he was making. Of course, he was exaggerating. That was obvious to both his parents, if it wasn't to him. But the fact was that the heart of it was true. He was being successful. He was making money. And he was happy.

So why wasn't she happy for him? Why wasn't she delighted that he was on the way to achieving his goal? Well, perhaps she was – a little. Of course she was pleased that he was making a success of the life he had set out for himself. But she was also worried. She was scared of the change that was taking place in him. She could see where the road was leading.

All the time it was just a dream that he could become rich, then that was what it was – just a dream. He talked about standing on people; he spoke about not caring who he had to step on in order to make his millions. What was it he used to say as he banged his fist on the table? 'I'm gonna make a million – and I don't care who I tread on as I do it.' But then it was just words. Now he seemed to mean it. He was making money and he didn't care who he trod upon as he did it.

The ancient Greeks told the legend of Narcissus, the son of

a river god. He was very good-looking and was
passionately loved by a nymph called Echo. But he had
fallen in love with his own reflection in the still water of a
spring. So he rejected Echo. The story ends with both
Narcissus and Echo pining away in frustration because of
their unfulfilled love.

As Andy told his stories, his mum noticed how characters appeared and then disappeared just as quickly. She wanted to say something to him. She wanted to talk to him about it. But she didn't know where to start. And she was a little afraid that, if she started on that subject, then she might cry or he might storm out.

So she sat, and she listened, and she smiled, and she tried to look impressed. Until she couldn't take it any more and so she interrupted him and said: 'Julia was asking about you again this week.'

Andy stopped and looked at her as if she had just arrived from another planet. *What on earth is she talking about. Whatever has that got to do with it?* he thought to himself.

If he could have read his mum's mind he would have known what it did have to do with it. He would have realised what it was that she was trying to do.

Julia had been a friend of Andy's for years. In fact, it wasn't long ago that they had seemed to be quite close. It all began when Andy had just come into the age when it is suddenly alright for a boy to have a girlfriend, and even to admit it to others. It was the age when most boys decide that kissing is not some wet disgusting thing that only gets in the way of the exciting action of a film – but is actually something that they quite like to experience for themselves.

It was at that time that Andy and Julia seemed to be

going out with one another. They walked home from school together, and they took a long time about it. When they arrived at Julia's home, just around the corner, they didn't quickly say goodbye. They went round the back, into the end of the lane that came out beside Julia's house, and there they stayed – sometimes for ages. Andy's mum was desperately curious to know what happened between them at the end of that lane. His dad suggested ways of finding out. But she contained her curiosity and she stopped him from playing one of his jokes. 'Whatever you do, don't embarrass the boy,' she said.

So he didn't. Andy's dad was the soul of discretion. He said nothing. He did nothing. Throughout the time that Andy appeared to be going out with Julia.

But that wasn't long. Because the relationship didn't last. They were clearly going in different directions. Andy had his sights set on money. Julia, on the other hand, just wanted to help people. She wasn't quite sure if she would train as a doctor or a nurse. That all depended upon the grades that she could achieve. But, whatever she did, she knew that she wanted to be a missionary.

Julia's father was the vicar of the local church and she had believed in God for as long as she could remember. It seemed to her that there never had been a time when she hadn't been aware of God. But it was only when she was about fifteen that she began to realise that just believing something was not enough. 'What's the point of believing something if it doesn't make any difference to your life?' her father had asked her one day. That question stuck in her mind for days. She heard it as she went to sleep, and again as she awoke. She knew that she had to answer it for herself. She had to decide what she was going to do with her life.

It was about that time that she decided to stop going out

with Andy. She had tried to persuade him of her beliefs. She had tried to help him think about his life and what he was going to do with it. For some time they talked about it every afternoon as they walked home from school. They would even sit for hours on the small bench at the end of the lane as they continued to argue about the purpose of life.

'You sound just like my mum,' Andy very often said to her.

'I'm sorry, I don't mean to.'

'Well you do. She's always on about this. I can't stand that about her. Dad's much better. He thinks like me.'

In fact Andy's dad didn't think like him very much at all – and he knew it. What he meant was that his dad didn't want anything to do with all that stuff about God. He never went with his wife as she headed off to church each Sunday. He just let her go on her own. Then when she came home he and Andy would be ready for her. It had become quite a regular Sunday occurrence. Andy had just got out of bed and his dad had finally finished reading the paper when his mum came home to face the ridicule. They didn't really want to be mean to her, it was just that they didn't want her passing any of the sermon on to them. So, under the principle that attack is the best form of defence, they attacked her. Not physically of course, but verbally, undermining her faith and ridiculing her beliefs.

So, when it came to his long sessions with Julia, Andy was well practised. He knew what to say. He knew where to attack. He could have done it blindfolded. The only problem was – he didn't really believe what he was saying. Whether he was joining forces with his dad against his mum or in single combat against Julia, Andy really wanted to be proved wrong. He wanted to find that they could answer his questions. He wanted to be convinced of a spiritual reality. But he never was. So, to him, the only reality was pounds and pence. 'If you can't add it up on a balance sheet I don't want to know about it,' he used to say to both Julia and his mum. The truth was that at the time he'd never seen a balance sheet and he didn't really know what one was. But they took the point, and so did he. They knew what he meant, and so did he.

With such a difference between them it was inevitable that Andy and Julia would pull apart. There was no dramatic teenage bust-up. They just went their separate ways. In time Andy went off to make his fortune in London, while Julia started training as a nurse. She opted to live at home during this time and so she saw Andy's mum most Sundays. She always asked how he was getting on. If Andy had actually phoned home any time that week, she would be told the latest news – which always interested her.

Andy, on the other hand, wasn't now the slightest bit interested to hear about Julia's life. As far as he was concerned she was part of the past, and best forgotten.

'Look, Mum,' he said, when she told him that Julia had been asking after him again. 'There are loads of girls in London, and they're a lot more interesting than Julia, I can tell you.'

'Oh,' said his mum.

She wanted to pursue the conversation but she was more than a little worried about what she might find out. She knew it didn't really make sense, but somehow she felt happier only guessing what Andy had been getting up to with the girls in London. She was pretty sure that she knew what he had been doing. And she knew that it didn't make any difference to the facts whether he told her or not. But it did make a difference to how she felt. She would rather not hear it from his lips. So she let the conversation

move straight back to Andy's talk of contracts and deals.
And she went back to sitting and smiling again.

Plato, the Greek philosopher, who was born in 428 BC, told a story of people who lived in a cave and were tied up at their hands and feet. All they ever saw were shadows on the wall, and all they ever heard were echoes of voices. So they thought that this was all that there was. And they became really absorbed in them. They held competitions and gave out prizes for those who could see the best shadows or hear the best echoes. Then one day one man became free and went out of the cave, into the real world. There for the first time he saw the sunshine and felt its warmth on his body. There, he began to experience a world that he never knew existed – a world of real people and real lives. That man went back into the cave and tried to tell the others about the world above – a world of real life and real sounds, not just shadows and echoes. But the others laughed at him, and mocked him. And Plato said, 'If anyone tried to loose another and lead him up to the light, let them only catch the offender, and they would put him to death.'

'Well, I'm going out now, Mum, see you later.' Andy hardly had time to draw a breath in between finishing his story and standing up to announce that he was off.

'Really?' said his dad.

'Where are you off to then?' asked his mum.

'Oh, just out, Mum,' he said. 'Look, when I'm in London you have no idea when I'm going out or coming back in. So don't worry about it just because I'm back here for a weekend. Don't crowd me, Mum.'

'I'm sorry,' she said. 'I was just interested to know, that was all.'

'Well, if you really need to know, I've arranged to meet some of my old friends in the Wheatsheaf.'

'Oh, that's nice. I'm glad you've done that,' said his mum.

'Nice' wasn't a word that Andy had in mind for the evening. Impressive, perhaps; alcoholic, certainly. But not 'nice'. Still, he didn't say anything. He didn't even say goodbye. He just grabbed his coat and left.

'You've got your key have you, son?' his dad called out as Andy climbed into his car.

'Yeah, of course I have,' came the reply. Andy was never really sure why he had kept his key to his parents' house when he had moved to London. But having it in his pocket was often comforting to him when he was under pressure in the office or feeling lonely in his room.

His old friends were already in the pub when Andy arrived. In fact it looked like they had been there for some time. They had pulled together two tables which were now covered with glasses, some full and others empty, as well as an assortment of empty crisp packets.

There were about fifteen of them altogether, gathered closely around the tables. They were here, like this, every Saturday night, sharing their stories of the week and catching up on their gossip. When Andy had phoned one of them from London he had been told that they always spent Saturday evening together in the Wheatsheaf. 'It's our way of keeping in touch,' he said. 'You don't want to lose good mates, do you?' Andy hadn't answered that question. He didn't really know what to say. He thought that it was a bit sad if all that they could think of doing on a Saturday night was sitting around chatting with the same group of people week in week out. Didn't they ever meet new people? Didn't they want to move on in their lives? Still, he was only going to be there for one night so he arranged that he would join them. 'Sure, Andy – come along,' he had been told.

So he did. He made an entrance. He thought it was a pretty impressive one. But it didn't seem to impress them. They looked up and said hello. They asked him how he was doing. They commented on the fact that he hadn't been around for a long time. But they didn't fall over him. They didn't treat him as the long-lost hero, or the brave explorer back from his adventures. In fact, it was difficult for Andy to break in to the group. They seemed to have pulled their chairs in tightly to one another like a circle of wagons set up to repel an Indian attack. He'd often seen it on a film, but never before experienced what it's like to be one of the Indians.

Andy went to the bar to get a drink. It was then that he noticed someone who had just bought her drink and was picking it up off the counter. He didn't recognise her at first, not from behind, her hair was done very differently. But as she turned round he saw immediately who it was. He hadn't expected that she would be there, of all places. He didn't think that this would be her scene. But she was clearly relaxed and comfortable there. As soon as she saw him she smiled, walked over, and gave him a gentle kiss on the cheek.

'Hello, Andy,' she said.

'Hello, Julia,' he replied.

She didn't take her drink back to the circle of chairs. She waited and stood with him as he ordered a pint of lager for himself. They began to talk together. It was a little slow and embarrassing at first. But as time passed they loosened up and began to speak to each other more freely. They each said, 'Well, I suppose we'd better go and sit down with the others,' several times. But they never did. In fact, they didn't move from that spot throughout the whole evening.

They saw the others periodically, each time they came up to the bar to refill their glasses. That gave Andy a chance to chat to them for a few moments, as they waited for the barman to serve them. They were very short conversations, only really long enough for him to think how sad and unambitious their lives seemed to be. In fact a few moments was all he wanted to spend talking to each of them. Even that was too much in some cases – they were so boring and predictable.

But Julia wasn't. Something about her sparkled, and he liked it. She had ambition, she had drive. She knew where she was heading in her life. She knew what she wanted to do with it. Andy didn't agree with her ambition at all, he didn't want to go where she was heading. But at least she was going somewhere. Throughout the evening Andy and Julia stood by the bar, facing each other, deep in conversation. For a moment it seemed like old times.

They argued and disagreed.

'I think what you need,' she said at one point, 'is to discover the spiritual side of life – you need God in your life.'

'Rubbish,' he replied. 'I'd rather have a pint of lager! The only spirit I want in my life comes in bottles.'

As they talked, and argued, and bantered, they hardly noticed the time passing. Andy couldn't even measure it by the number of pints he drank. Julia seemed to get through her glass very slowly and he felt uncomfortable refilling his more often than her, so he drank much less than he had become used to in his time in London.

At the end of the evening, when the barman called 'time' and the room gradually emptied, Andy was not drunk as he had been so often recently. He even thought that it would be alright for him to drive home. It wasn't very far, and he could probably make it. He'd be OK.

He didn't need to bring the car in the first place – he

only took it down there because he thought his friends would be keen to see it. Which they weren't. And now he had to get it home somehow.

'I'll give you a lift home, shall I?' Andy asked Julia as they drained the last of the drink from their glasses and put them down on the bar amongst the forest of others.

'No way,' she said, 'not after the amount you've drunk. Come on, we'll walk home. You can leave the car overnight and pick it up in the morning.'

Andy protested that she was acting like his mum again. But he didn't complain too much. He let himself be persuaded by her. Because, in fact, he really wanted to walk home with her anyway. They left the pub and were soon on the same route that they had used every day during that time when they had walked home from school together. They walked in the same way. They talked in the same way. When they arrived back at Julia's house they even went around the back to the small lane, where they sat on the bench and continued their discussion in the same way.

It was very late when they finally stood up and walked out of the lane towards the front of Julia's house. Andy didn't quite know what to do at that point. He wanted to kiss her. In fact he wanted to do far more than that. But he couldn't. They hadn't touched each other all evening – apart from the little 'hello' kiss Julia had given him on his cheek when they first met. Since then all they had done was to talk. It wasn't as if there was anything romantic that had developed between them. Well, not anywhere other than in Andy's mind anyway. Given half a chance he would have taken her in his arms there and then, and taken her back to the bench where he could show her how to really enjoy herself. But he knew that wasn't an option, not with Julia. So he said, 'Goodnight,' lent over and gave

her a small kiss on her cheek. She smiled, turned round
and went in.

> *. . . everything can be taken from a man but one thing: the*
> *last of the human freedoms – to choose one's attitude in any*
> *given set of circumstances, to choose one's own way.*
>   Victor Frankel (*Man's Search for Meaning*, 1963)

> *The universe is a sad place, a lonely place.*
>   Catherine Vautan, *I* ❤ *Huckabees*
>   (Twentieth Century Fox, 2004)

7

I guess I was always scared that people would leave me. Each night, as I lay in bed trying to get to sleep, I found that nothing could stop the nagging doubt that, when I woke up, Mum wouldn't be there any more. I was terrified that she was going to leave us again. And even in the morning, when I found that she was still there, I knew that Dad would leave us that evening anyway – as he did every evening. Well, his body was still there of course, but he was drunk, so it wasn't really him, it was someone else – he had gone away again.

More than anything else in the world I wanted to know that there was someone who would be with me for ever and who would never leave me. I wanted someone I could trust, someone I could rely upon.

I tried to find this in friendships at school. But that is never easy for anyone. Kids seems to fall in and out of friendship every day. Attachments seem to be constantly changing. Most kids cope with that very well, but then I guess I wasn't like most kids. I needed security and stability around me. I needed to know that I belonged, and I never felt that I did. I was the girl from the outside, the one with the second-hand clothes and the cut down shoes. I was an embarrassment. They didn't want to be seen with me.

Things began to change when I moved into some different classes at school. We had just sat some exams and we were then put into new groups for some of our lessons. Strangely enough I had done really well and got some good grades. I don't know how, because it was so hard to work and revise at home. Anyway I got high enough marks to be put in the top set for some subjects – and that was the start of my friendship with Jenny.

She was a tall girl with long dark hair, high cheek bones and a clear complexion. Quite a beauty in fact. When the rest of us were struggling desperately with the onset of spots, Jenny didn't seem to have any problem at all. I would wake up each morning and run to the mirror to check what damage there was on my face that day – and figure out ways of covering up the newest crop of erupting volcanoes. But Jenny didn't seem to have to worry about that. Her face always looked clear, and clean, and beautiful.

She was also very clever, and full of fun. So, inevitably, she was very popular. The other girls liked her, they liked being with her and they loved to bask in her reflected beauty.

I don't know how I ended up sitting next to her. That was just where the teacher put me when I moved into the new classes. Anyway, from the first moment I sat down Jenny was friendly to me. She smiled at me, and we chatted. When we should have been working we chattered, when the lesson was over we chattered.

As the weeks went by, we spent even more time together. We found that there was a natural bond between us. Despite the fact that she now had a clear southern accent, she was really a northerner. She had been brought up just outside Nottingham, and her parents had moved down south when she was at primary school. Her dad was something to do with electricity. She didn't really know, and I didn't really care. The fact was that they were northerners, they were like me, and I was really pleased to say yes when Jenny asked me to go home with her for tea one day.

Jenny's mum was very much like mine. She was loud and brash, she didn't hide things behind a southern front, everything was out in the open with her. She loved having people in her house and she made a real fuss of me, giving me cakes and biscuits – more than even I could pack in at one go. I was still there when her dad came home. And I couldn't believe how much he was like mine – well, my daytime Dad anyway. He was strong and stocky, and full of fun. He didn't come in quietly and then hide away behind a paper, like the southern dads seemed to do. Once he had arrived home you knew it – everyone knew it. And he didn't ignore me. As soon as he found out that Jenny had brought a friend home he came bursting into her room where she and I were trying out our make-up, and introduced himself to me, and said how welcome I was in the house and how I could come any time I wanted and how any friend of Jenny's is a friend of his and . . . he didn't leave until Jenny's mum called us all down to the table.

That was the first of many times I ate with Jenny at her house. She also came back to my place and found that she got on quite well with my parents too. She didn't notice that we didn't have all the things that she had in her house, or that the things we did have were mostly broken. Well, she didn't seem to notice anyway – or if she did then she didn't care. Anyway, after the first few visits I stopped feeling worried or embarrassed about her coming in. I relaxed. I felt stable and secure in my friendship with her.

For me, Jenny was not just a new friend, she was also a

doorway to many other new friends. Because she was popular, I became more popular. When she went out with a group of girls, I went along too. When she suggested that a group of us went to the cinema, I was included amongst them.

Within the space of a few months my social life seemed to turn around completely. I had friends, I had places to go with them – and I had money to spend when I was there.

Well, I had some money anyway. I started my first small job around that time. I worked in the local post-office for a few hours, two days a week. It was quite simple work, mainly selling cards to old ladies and sweets to the local school-kids. It wasn't much effort – and there wasn't much pay. But for the first time I had some money in my pocket.

It was around that time that a group of us started going down town together on a Saturday morning. I really loved that. Every week I went to Jenny's house to call for her, and then we walked into the centre, where we met up with the others. Sometimes it would be just four of five of us, at other times it was even more. We spent most of the time in clothes shops looking at the latest fashions, and trying them on. Jenny always looked the best in them of course, but I occasionally found some items that suited me. It was then that the other girls would encourage me to buy them.

'Go on, it looks great on you,' they would say. 'Just get it – it may not still be here next week.'

I suppose that it didn't take much to persuade me. After all, I'd spent the last few years listening to the same girls giggle about me because of my second-hand clothes – and now they were telling me how good I looked in this skirt, or top, or dress.

So, most weeks, I bought something. They usually cost more money than I had. But that wasn't a problem because the other girls lent me money to cover the difference. I never asked them. They just offered.

'You've got to get it,' they would say. 'Look, I'll lend you the money. You can pay me back later.'

So I borrowed from them. And each week I borrowed more. Sometimes from the same girls, sometimes from others. I couldn't see any problem with this. For once they were being kind to me and helping me out. And I was earning money so I would be able to pay them back.

As the weeks went by it never occurred to me that the other girls might be getting a bit annoyed that I was continuing to borrow money from them, and wasn't paying any back. I couldn't really see how it would bother them – because they always seemed to have loads of money. Their families were very rich – and no matter how much they lent me, they always had plenty more.

I suppose that I should have picked up the signs. But you don't when you're so happy. I had a new group of friends, and new clothes, and new jewellery. We had fun together. We enjoyed shopping together. I didn't notice that they had stopped offering to lend me money. I simply had got used to it. And I expected it. So, when I saw something that I liked, I simply asked one of them, 'Can you lend me the money for this?'

I didn't even notice how much more reluctant they were to hand me their cash. I did sometimes feel a bit puzzled by the fact that they would suddenly tell me that they didn't have any more, when I knew full well that they still had some in their pocket. But even then I didn't realise what had happened.

If only I had. If only I had stopped borrowing and paid them back. I would have been spared the pain and humiliation that I faced that Monday morning.

For some reason they didn't wait for me as I packed my books away after the morning lessons. A group of us usually hung around for one another and then went off together to sit somewhere and wait for our lunch-bell. But that day they all packed away very quickly and I was left behind. I didn't know where they had gone. We never had one particular place where we always hung out – we would drift around different places in the school.

Anyway, on that Monday I searched for them around the corridors and out in the fields, but they weren't there. I had just about given up when I thought that I would try behind the Maths block. There was a corner of a wall there that we had sometimes sat on or leant against as we talked about boys or make-up.

It was as I walked down the path towards the Maths block that I began to hear them. They were voices I recognised. It was my friends, and they were talking. As I drew closer I began to make out what they were saying. They weren't talking about boys or make-up or even TV or music. They were talking about me.

'She's such a scrounger. I hate it.'

'It's so embarrassing. Why does she think that she can just take our money whenever she wants to?'

'I didn't mind at first – but now it's just going on and on.'

'She wants everything for free.'

'She doesn't want to pay for anything.'

'I hate her.'

'Me too.'

I froze to the spot. My stomach felt as if someone was stretching it down inside me, pulling at it, clawing at it.

And do you know what was the worst thing? It was the fact that I recognised one voice in particular. It was Jenny's. She was the one who said that I was a scrounger. She was the one who said, 'I hate her.' In fact she was the one who seemed to be leading them as they tore me apart with their words.

I closed my eyes and tried to keep the tears inside, but they escaped between the lids. I felt the sense of abandonment and loneliness as it poured back into me. I guess it's only when you lose something that you realise how precious it has been. For the past few months I had not been scared that people would leave me. I had not even lain awake at night wondering whether Mum was going to go again. I had felt secure and stable. But now those good feelings had gone. And they were replaced once more with the all too familiar sense of fear and loneliness.

Even now, years later, I can still remember exactly how I felt at that point. In some ways I can still experience it. People say that time is a great healer. But it's not, not really. Time is a great redecorator. It papers over the cracks and paints over the fault lines. But they're still there, under the surface. If you peel my paper away you will still see the marks and the scars.

The biggest disease today is not leprosy or tuberculosis, but rather the feeling of being unwanted, uncared for and deserted by everybody.
Mother Theresa of Calcutta (1910–1997)

You may run from sorrow, as we have. . . Sorrow will find you.
August Nicholson, *The Village*
(Touchstone Pictures, 2004)

* * *

Sharon was wide awake as soon as she opened her eyes. It was a great new day and she threw back the blanket as far as it would go. She stood up and looked at herself in the mirror. She looked good, she felt good. She was strong. She was powerful.

She spent the morning trying out different poses and different facial expressions. She washed her hair and put on her make-up. Eventually it was time to leave for the studio.

This time she was early. She knocked on the door, but it wasn't open and she had to wait for quite a while before she heard the sound of the key turning in the lock.

'Yeah?' said the balding lanky man who opened the door. 'What is it?'

'Um, I've come to, um, model for James.'

The man said nothing as he took a cigarette from behind his ear and lit it. When he had taken a deep drag he stepped back from the doorway and said, 'You're early – you must be keen.'

He left the door open as he turned his back on her and walked across the studio to his camera equipment.

Sharon hesitated. She wasn't quite sure what to do. Then she saw a woman over in the corner by the rack of clothes. She was getting dressed, and as she turned round she smiled at her. Sharon smiled back and picked her way across the studio towards her.

'Hi, I'm Karen, I'm just finishing. Who are you?'

'I'm Sharon, I'm a bit early.'

'Sharon – I haven't heard about you. You're new, are you?'

'Yeah, just started yesterday.'

'Oh, I see. That must have been with James then.'

'Yeah, that's right.'

'I thought so,' said Karen. 'I've had him. Most do when they start. But right now I've got old Stephen there. He's a right pain.'

Sharon looked up to see the photographer picking up the last of his bags of camera equipment and swinging them over his shoulder, as he headed for the door. 'Thank goodness for that,' she said as she watched him leave. 'For a minute I thought James was off sick or something and he was gonna take my photos.'

'No, James will be here soon. He's often late. Mind you, you will have Stephen eventually. Everyone does. In fact all of them have all of us eventually. They sort of pass us around. Trying us out – you know what I mean? Anyway, look, I've got to go. I've got to pick up my kids from school. We'll meet again, I'm sure we will. We'll probably do some shoots together before long. Yeah, looking at you I'd rather have you than some of the others.'

Karen had put on the last of her clothes and walked across the studio as she was speaking, and before Sharon could ask her any of the questions that were bubbling up in her mind she was gone. Sharon was left on her own in the studio.

She didn't know quite what to do. For a while she just stood still and looked around. There wasn't much to see. She had seen most of it yesterday. She thought that she might as well go and sit down on the plastic chairs in the corner by the kitchen area. As she walked towards them she noticed a pile of photographs stacked roughly on the top of the fridge.

Sharon walked past the chairs and over to the fridge. Gingerly she picked up some of the photos and looked at them. They were photos of Karen. And she wasn't just topless. She was showing everything, absolutely everything. Sharon was shocked. She had seen photos like that before, of course. The lads on the estate often had magazines that they passed around. But somehow she hadn't made the connection between what she was doing in the studio and what the boys looked at in the magazines. She closed her eyes and felt stupid. For a moment she thought that perhaps she should just leave. Forget all about it. Go back to the café and back to sharing the room with Sue.

But somehow she couldn't face that. So she opened her

eyes and looked again at the photos. She concentrated on Karen's face, on her expression. She wondered what it felt like for her as she posed like that. And she thought of her now, outside the school gates, waiting to pick up her kids.

'That's where the big money is.'

Sharon recognised the voice and turned around to see James coming through the door with his bags of camera equipment. 'I said, that's how you make the real money,' he repeated.

Sharon didn't know quite what to say. When James had put down his last bag she asked quietly, 'How much?'

'Well,' said James, 'at least four times as much as you are going to get for this shoot today.'

'Really?'

'Yeah. It's easy money. What's the difference? It's no harder showing everything than just showing your top. Actually it's easier, because you don't have to keep making sure that bits of you are covered up. No, it's really easy money. And if you get a job like that, showing pink, then you can get even more.'

Sharon wanted to ask what he meant by 'showing pink' but didn't want to appear stupid, and thought she could guess anyway.

'I'll talk to the agency if you like and see if we can get you some more money this afternoon. What do you reckon?' James smiled at her as he waited for her answer.

'No, I don't think so,' she said eventually. 'Let's just do the same as yesterday.'

'OK,' said James. 'Here's the money, I'll put it here on the table, then you can look at it as you're posing. But before we start I've got to get you to sign this form. You can't do anything without the dreaded paper-work these days.'

James took out an old brown envelope from his camera bag and extracted a sheet of paper which was covered with small print. 'Right, I need you to sign here and to date it,' he said as he pointed to the box at the bottom.

'But what is it?' Sharon asked.

'It's just a standard form that enables the publisher to get the photos on to calendars and posters and things. You're gonna be a star.'

'Do I have to sign this?' Sharon asked.

'Of course you do. Every time you do a photo shoot you'll have to sign an assignment form like this. You won't get paid otherwise.'

'But I haven't been paid.'

'I know you haven't, not for yesterday anyway. That was just trying you out and seeing if you could do it. A lot of girls can't, you know. The agency are supposed to send us only girls who are able to do this. But you'd be amazed how many can't hack it. I've seen loads run out that door. You know I could tell . . .'

James stopped suddenly, and wished he could take back his last few sentences. He waited and watched Sharon to see what she would do.

She didn't do anything for a moment, but then she suddenly grabbed the form and signed it in the box.

'Right,' she said, 'let's earn that money.'

Over the following two hours Sharon wore half a dozen different outfits. Some of which she liked, some of which she hated. But in all of which she posed and pouted.

James said much less than he had the day before. He hardly ever said 'Great' or 'Super' or 'Excellent'. When he did talk it was usually to tell her how he wanted her to stand, or sit, or lie down. He was very particular about the shots he wanted and he spent a long time lining them up. Sometimes he got quite cross with her because she didn't know exactly what he wanted.

So everything took much longer than it had the

previous day. The shutter clicked much less frequently. And Sharon noticed how often James had to stop and change the film – something she couldn't remember him doing at all the previous day.

Sharon was young and she was new to this whole business. But she wasn't stupid. She could work it out. And she knew what was required of her. She knew what she had to do. And she knew that she could do it. She was hard. She could cope.

And she did. Of course she didn't enjoy it at all. Not like she had before. She missed all the attention that James had given her. But most of all she missed the sense of power. She was standing provocatively, and acting seductively, in fact she was doing everything that James told her to do. But it was no longer her in charge. He was the one with the power. He was in control.

It came as a surprise when he finally put down the camera and joined her on the couch. She hadn't expected it. She wasn't ready for it. She didn't want it. But, then, she was used to that. After all, it was just like another night at home. She was powerless to stop it. There was no point resisting. Obviously this was her fault too. She had been acting seductively, she had been provocative. What else did she expect him to do? She lay still. She tried not to move. She wanted to pull the blanket up and over her head. She thought to herself, *I can cope, I'm well 'ard.*

In pornography the pleasure of the women expressed in it is fake and the violence against them is real.

Catharine MacKinnon, Michigan University
(quoted in *The Sunday Times*, September 1998)

8

*There is a story told of a nobleman who overheard his
servant crying. Between his sobs he heard him say, 'I wish
I had £50, if only I had £50 then I would be happy.' The
nobleman thought to himself what a good servant this man
had been. So he went over to him and said, 'I overheard you
crying. I could hear you saying "If only I had £50," so I
have decided to give you that £50. I want you to be happy.'
The servant was amazed, he didn't know what to say. But
as he watched the nobleman walk away he said to himself,
'If only I'd cried out for £100.'*

Andy didn't sleep much that night. He was troubled and
puzzled by his reaction to Julia. He didn't quite know
what to make of it. He was still mulling it over in his mind
the next morning as he walked into town to collect his car.
He tried to get thoughts of Julia out of his mind as he
drove back to his parents' house.

But the route took him past Julia's dad's church. For
some reason he couldn't just drive past it. He stopped the
car outside and turned off the engine. He must have sat
there for half an hour, thinking, wondering what he
should do. He looked at the church door and thought of
Julia, who was somewhere inside. No matter how much

If Only

he tried, he couldn't understand it. What was she doing in there? Why was she wasting her life in a stuffy old building full of stuffy old ladies in hats? For a moment he thought of bursting in, sweeping her up in his arms and carrying her off in his sports car – to a new exciting life in London. But then he realised he had just been watching too many corny films. Eventually, reluctantly, he started his car and pulled away.

When he arrived at his parents' house he found his dad, sat in his usual chair, just finishing the paper. Andy sat down opposite him and waited. His mum would be home soon. Now he, and his dad, were ready – again. He didn't see Julia that day, although he wanted to. He spent the afternoon with his mum and dad, trying not to argue too much, before he packed his car and headed back to London.

As he drove he planned, in his mind, that he would go back to his parents' again quite soon. And when he did, he would arrange to see Julia.

In the months and years that followed, Andy went back many times. Sometimes Julia wasn't around, but usually she was. They spent many hours walking and talking together. They never touched each other, apart from their, now customary, little kiss on the cheek. Julia had made it quite clear that she wasn't interested in that kind of a relationship. Andy found it hard to understand her attitude. How could she just want to be friends, and nothing more? The girls in London that he met at the various pubs and clubs would do plenty of the 'more' without any of the friendship stuff. But Julia was the other way round. He couldn't figure it.

However, he didn't let this emotional turmoil get in the way of his work. During those years Andy had regular visits to the personnel office, where he was told that, once again, he had been promoted to another level. This always meant an increase in his salary – and it often entailed a move up to another floor in the office block.

Every time he moved there were new people to meet – and old ones to forget. Each office gave the impression of being a community, where people worked together and shared together. But it wasn't a real community. These were pretend friends who worked together for the time they were in the same office – until they moved on to the next one.

The less a man is forced to come into contact with others, the better off he is.

Arthur Schopenhauer (1788–1860)

If I had goodness, I lost it. If I had anything tender in me, I shot it dead.

Inman, *Cold Mountain* (Miramax, 2003)

For most of the time this seemed to suit Andy. He didn't want to get bogged down with people. He was on the move. He was on the way up. He had become the master of the three-month friendship. No sooner had he got to know people than he would forget them and move on to the next group.

But there were times when this took its toll on him. There were times when he wondered where he belonged. Not just in the office, but also in life. Sometimes he felt rootless and alone – as if he had just arrived on the planet and didn't really belong here.

Sometimes he also felt the strain of it all. At one point he wondered if there might be something wrong with him. He had just been promoted yet again, and was working long hours staring at rows of figures. But as each day progressed he found it harder to concentrate. His head ached. It wasn't the kind of pain that he was used to in the morning after a heavy night's drinking. This was something different. It didn't wear off. If anything it got worse through the day.

For a while he was worried about himself. Was he over-doing it? Was he working too hard? What was he doing to his body? Andy made an appointment with the doctor. He almost cancelled it several times but the headaches weren't getting any better so he knew he would have to go. The doctor listened to Andy's story and didn't take long checking him over before suggesting that, instead of coming to him, Andy should have made an appointment at the optician's.

He felt such a fool as he left. Why had he worried about himself like that? What did he think he was – some wimp who couldn't stand the pace of hard work? He could cope with it. He could manage anything – all he had to do was sort out his eyes. Within days he had been to the optician and a week later he picked up his glasses. From then on Andy threw himself into his work with a new energy and enthusiasm. As long as he had his glasses he could do anything, work any hours, cope with any pressure.

Others spurred him on with his determination to succeed – particularly Geoff Phillips. He was at least thirty years older than Andy, and had worked very hard to get where he was. He had risen up through the ranks of the business world in the same way that Andy intended to do. He hadn't let anything hold him back. Not even his family. Well, he and his wife were divorced now anyway and he hadn't seen his children for years, so they couldn't get in his way anyhow.

In Japan many people are working so hard that they lose touch with their family. So, one enterprising company has produced a solution. In Tokyo you can dial the offices of the Nippon Kokasei Honbu who will rent you a family by the hour. You might ask for a daughter, a son-in-law and a couple of grandchildren to come and spend time with you. Soon after, some actors will turn up at your door and greet you emotionally as if you have not seen them for years. Three hours cost $1,130 plus transport.

World Press Review, Vol. 39, No. 8, 1992

There it is, that little itch you need to scratch. Always about the money . . . So who cares if you have to bend the rules a little bit, so long as nobody gets hurt. Then somebody does.

Jake Vig, *Confidence* (Lion's Gate Films, 2004)

Geoff had spotted Andy some while ago, and realised that he was someone who did good work reliably. So he engineered it that Andy would work with him on particular projects. Consequently they were usually completed ahead of schedule and Geoff looked good in the eyes of the promotion board. The relationship worked well, and so Geoff did everything he could to develop and train his young protégé.

All of this took place in the days before 'mentoring' had become a trendy word used in management-speak. But mentoring was exactly what was taking place. Geoff mentored Andy in the office – and in the bar. He was well known as a heavy drinker. He could put away more than most people. He not only drank a lot after work, but also at lunchtime. And now he also took Andy with him.

It was during those lunchtime drinking sessions that Andy would ask Geoff questions about work or about life.

'You've got to realise that everyone's got their price,' Geoff told him.

'What, bribery, you mean?' asked Andy.

'Well, yes and no. There's a lot of bribery in any kind of business – but it's not usually grubby pound notes passed over in beaten-up old suitcases. It's much more sophisticated than that.'

'Like what then?' enquired Andy.

'Well, take us for instance. Think of the hours we work. Think of the things we have given up in order to be successful.'

It was the first time that Geoff had ever indicated that he might have given things up, and made sacrifices in his life in order to get where he was. Andy said nothing, but lent across towards him, waiting for him to continue.

'Well, we've taken a bribe, haven't we? A whacking great pay cheque at the end of each month. You see, everyone has their price.'

It was during one of the regular lunchtime drinking sessions that Andy asked a question that he had never asked before. Of course it had been on his mind for months, since that first time he went home and met Julia again. But he had never felt that he could ask Geoff about it – until he had talked about the sacrifices he had made.

'Do you ever wonder . . .?' he started.

'What?' Geoff interrupted.

'Do you ever wonder whether there might be anything more to life than this? Do you ever think about spiritual questions?'

'Well, sorry mate, you're asking the wrong person here. I try not to think about it too much. And I suggest that you don't think about it either. All I know is what I see – this world around. Do I know if there is anything more? Do I care!'

Geoff laughed out loud. And Andy tried to laugh along with him.

I proclaim that I believe in nothing and everything is absurd.

Albert Camus (1913–1960)

Why do people only ask deep questions when something bad happens, and then forget them?

Tommy, *I* ❤ *Huckabees*
(Twentieth Century Fox, 2004)

'Look, let's get back to reality. We've got a lot of work to do on this Wingate Report. The deadline's rushing up and we've never missed one before, have we? So let's get on and get this done. I need you to compile all those figures – and I'll write the text. We'll get it done this afternoon, however long it takes, and then we'll meet up at lunchtime tomorrow here. We'll have a few beers and we'll go over it together.'

'OK,' said Andy.

'Call me first thing in the morning, will you, to confirm the lunchtime meeting. I don't want to put it off, but you know what my diary is like these days.'

'Fine,' Andy replied.

'OK, let's just have another quick one before we head back, shall we?'

Andy wanted to say no, but he couldn't. After all, Geoff was his mentor.

That afternoon Geoff worked as hard as he could writing the text for the report. As the hours passed his head gradually cleared and the work flowed more quickly. He stayed late into the evening, but when he had finally finished it, there were still a few other lights on in the offices on his floor. Geoff knocked on a few doors to find

If Only

out if any of them fancied a few drinks with him in the lounge bar of the Crown Hotel. One of them decided to call it a day and go with him. They didn't know each other very well, but each was pleased to have someone else to drink with.

After their third or fourth drink – Geoff never did keep a count of the rounds – he told his drinking mate of the question that Andy had asked him that lunch-time.

'Really?' the man said.

'Yeah,' replied Geoff

They both laughed.

Geoff continued drinking on the train that took him home. 'Home' wasn't a word that he liked to use very much. He had a house that he lived in. It was a very expensive house in an exclusive area south of London. It had an impressive portico above the large front door. But inside the house was empty. Of course it had furniture in it, and cabinets and beds. But it had no soul, no life about it. The chairs were rarely sat upon. The bed was only slept in for short periods. The cooker was hardly ever turned on. The only piece of furniture that was used as much as the manufacturers had intended was the drinks cabinet.

It was to this cabinet that Geoff immediately went as soon as he came in, that night and every night. Sometimes it was just a quick drink before he went to bed, other times he would work his way through a bottle. That night was one of those. He pulled out the flagon of whisky and a glass – and settled down to drink himself into oblivion.

He felt that he deserved it. In fact he really felt that he needed it that night because he didn't seem to be very well. He'd been feeling a bit strange all day. He'd been a bit breathless and he had a nagging pain down his arm and across his chest. *The best thing to do*, he thought to himself, *is to drink it away.*

So he did. In the morning he had no idea how he had got up to the bedroom the night before. But he'd obviously got himself there somehow, and it was there on his bed where he now lay – listening to the incessant clatter of his alarm clock.

Geoff felt terrible. His head hurt. His chest ached. And his mouth felt as if someone had stuffed an old dry sock into it. All he wanted to do was to lie there and sleep it off. But that wasn't possible. Somehow he had to get himself into the office. And somehow he did. He managed to shower and shave, and catch the train.

When he eventually sat down at his desk he felt worse than he ever had in his life before. He couldn't remember a time when he had been as bad as this. In fact he couldn't remember much about his life at all. He wasn't even quite sure who he was anymore. Or where he was. He tried to look around, but everything seemed to be dark around him – as if someone had switched off all the lights. He tried to call out, but he couldn't say anything. He couldn't even make a noise. All he could feel was the pain. All he could do was to try to breathe. But then he couldn't even do that any more. Or hold up his head, or his body, which fell forwards on to his desk, still and lifeless.

No man can avoid reaching the end of his life
　　　　Ed Bloom, *Big Fish* (Columbia Tristar, 2003)

The simple truth is not all of us become the men we once hoped we might be.
　　　　Jack Aubrey, *Master and Commander:*
Far Side of the World (Twentieth Century Fox, 2003)

* * *

Dr David Cook, a British philosopher, tells the story of a man who meets a woman and asks her, 'Will you sleep with me if I give you a million pounds?' She thinks for a while and replies, 'OK then, I will.' He then says, 'No, I want to change that. Will you sleep with me if I give you one pound?' 'Certainly not,' she replies immediately, 'what kind of a woman do you think I am?' 'Oh,' he says, 'I thought we'd already established that; all we are doing now is haggling about the price.'

Sharon had a bit of time before her appointment at The Majestic Model Agency. So she decided that she would stop off at the newsagent, on the way, to buy some cigarettes and chocolate. She liked that – being able to decide to buy something and knowing that she had enough money in her pocket to pay for it. Of course that shoot hadn't given her as much as Karen must have made for hers. But it was more than she earned in a whole week in the café, and it was all over in a few hours. Finished. Completed. So what if it had ended in the way it had. She was hard. She could cope.

And now she had enough money in her pocket to buy as many cigarettes and chocolates as she wanted. Well, as much as she wanted for that day anyway. For today she was free to buy anything, to do anything. Perhaps she would buy some sweets. Or, better still, a fashion or style magazine. She still hadn't quite given up the idea of being a fashion model – despite the fact that they had told her she was too short.

'Yeah,' she said to herself, 'I'll pick up a magazine as well.'

She had never really noticed them before. But she reckoned that they must have often been there – these men who stood at the magazine rack flicking through the pornographic magazines. But when she saw them this time she stopped. She could easily have squeezed through and looked at the fashion magazines. But, for some reason, she didn't feel able to.

Sharon wasn't sure what she thought. She felt confused. Through her eyes she could see the men steadily turning the pages. But in her mind she could see Karen, getting changed, and setting off to pick up her kids from school.

Did these men ever think about the girls in the photos? Sharon wondered to herself. *Do they realise that these are real girls with real lives, real hopes and real dreams? Do they realise that these girls have real feelings? Or do they? Can they?*

For a while Sharon just stood there, lost in thought. She was thinking about her own life, her own feelings. She thought about the nights in her bed, with the blanket pulled over her. She thought about her feelings of numbness.

Suddenly she was disturbed by one of the men who had turned round and was pushing past her. She watched as he paid for two magazines. She saw the notes he handed over.

Sharon never bought her fashion magazine and she didn't bother getting the chocolates either. She left the shop with only a packet of cigarettes which she opened straight away.

By the time she arrived at the agency she had finished two cigarettes and made up her mind.

'I've seen the photos,' the small balding man said. 'I knew you'd be good. Now are you ready for some real work?'

'I reckon I am,' Sharon replied.

'You know what I mean?'

'Yeah. I do,' said Sharon 'I can cope. Anything – whatever.'

'Right,' he said, 'now we're talking. Let's book some dates.'

Over the weeks that followed, Sharon learned to play the game. She knew what the photographers wanted, she knew what the readers needed, and she gave it to them. It was hard at first, of course it was, but the more she did it, the easier it became.

She made quite a bit of money and spent a lot of it in the Rising Sun. She found it very easy to fit in – particularly with the biker gang. She liked being around them, especially Tony. In fact it wasn't long before Tony staked his claim on her and told the other bikers that she was now his.

Almost immediately she moved in with him. He shared a house with some of his mates and he was keen to have his new young trophy with him. Sharon was also keen – because it meant that she could get away from Sue. She didn't want to have to share the room with her any more. They had grown apart again very quickly – rather like they did when they moved from primary to secondary school. They didn't really have anything in common with each other any more.

Sharon moved out as soon as she could – when Sue wasn't around. She didn't wait to say anything. She didn't really know what to say. She did leave a small note and a big box of chocolates to say thank you as best she could. But that was all. She never saw Sue again. Well, she wouldn't expect to. After all, Sue wasn't the kind of person who would go to the Rising Sun. And it was there that Sharon now spent most of her time.

Over those weeks Sharon also began to get to know Karen. They met several times as they crossed each other at the studio. They always took the opportunity to talk and there seemed to be a natural affinity between them. So, one day, when Karen's photographer didn't show up, Sharon suggested that they should go out for a coffee together.

She liked Karen. She could talk to her. And she could ask her questions that she didn't feel that she could ask anyone else. It was Karen who told her that the way in which the photo sessions often ended for Sharon was the same for her and all the girls. She told her that the photographers saw it as a perk of the job. You couldn't say no. If you did then they would complain that you were a difficult model and you wouldn't get any more work.

'But that's outrageous,' said Sharon. 'It's immoral.'

'So who are we to talk about morals.'

'But it's like being a prostitute.'

'Yeah, it certainly feels like that. The photographers use us, then the publishers use us, then the guys who use the magazines use us. Everybody uses us. But who cares? You can't cope if you care.'

And Sharon knew what she meant. She didn't care. Not any more. That just wasn't her. Whoever 'her' was. She wasn't really sure that she recognised herself any more. Whoever she was now she certainly wasn't the same little girl who had won the primary school prize for 'the most helpful child'. That was someone else, someone who couldn't play the game that she played now.

'You know what?' said Karen. 'I sometimes think about doing it that way anyway.'

'What do you mean?' asked Sharon.

'Well, they pay us to take photos of us, then they reckon they have the right to sleep with us for nothing. So why not become an escort and get paid for it properly?'

'Would you really do that?' Sharon asked as she put down her coffee mug and leant across the table.

'Yeah, of course I would. Why not?'

'But wouldn't you feel . . . feel . . . No, I suppose you wouldn't.'

Sharon narrowed her eyes and thought, while Karen looked at her quizzically.

'I wonder what's it like, then, doing escort work?'

'I dunno. I've never done it. But I reckon it's no different to what I was going to be doing with the photographer right now if he had turned up. Except that when it's all over it's all over, if you know what I mean. There's no pictures, no more men doing it to you again and again.'

'You know what,' said Sharon, 'you make it sound like a good career move.'

Karen laughed.

9

Time is chasing after all of us.
J.M. Barrie, *Finding Neverland*
(Buena Vista, 2004)

Geoff's death hit Andy hard. He didn't really know how to cope with it. It wasn't that he had never known anyone who had died, or never seen anyone die, for that matter. In fact Geoff's was the third death that had taken place in or around their office block in the past month. But that was precisely what made Andy think about it so much. He had seen or heard about all of them as they died. One minute they were there, the next they were gone. But where had they gone to? What happens when we die? What are we living for in the first place anyway?

The questions raced around Andy's head. They wouldn't stop. Even if he tried to immerse himself in his work, or to drown himself in lager. Nothing seemed to make any difference. These were big questions and he had to find an answer.

That night Andy phoned Julia and told her that he would be coming home at the weekend. He asked her if she would like to go with him on one of their walks. The answer was yes – as Andy expected that it would be. But he had another question too and he didn't really know how to put it. He hesitated for a while. But he couldn't hold it in.

'Julia,' he said.

'Yes?'

'Can I come to church with you on Sunday?'

'Of course you can. It will be lovely to have you. I've often . . .'

'Now hang on a second, Julia,' Andy interrupted her, 'don't make a fuss. And don't say anything about it to my mum or dad, will you – especially Dad. I've just got some questions that I want to think through, that's all.'

'OK. That's fine,' she said.

So that Sunday Andy went into the church for the first time. Julia met him outside – when he eventually came. He was late and the service had already started.

'Can we just slip in at the back?' he asked.

'Sure,' she replied, and led him through the doors to a pew in the back corner.

Andy didn't look around as he walked in; he felt embarrassed and really didn't want anyone to see him, especially not his mother. But once he had sat down, with Julia next to him, he looked up – and was very surprised by what he saw. For a start the church was quite full – he'd never expected that. But the thing that amazed him most of all was the number of young people that were there. And they weren't just young girls, there were lots of lads as well. Many of them were about his age, he even saw a few he recognised.

He listened to the service, and tried to find something that would help him to answer his questions. But he couldn't. The vicar was talking about some things that Andy didn't understand at all – even a lot of the words were ones he hadn't heard before. So he gave up listening and started looking around. It was then that he noticed the people's faces. He couldn't see them very well from his seat at the back. But he was able to catch sight of them when he looked over to the side, or people turned round a bit. And he was struck by their expressions. They clearly had something about them – something like the sparkle that he had first really noticed in Julia's face that Saturday night in the Wheatsheaf. He couldn't say what it was, but they had some kind of peace and joy that he wasn't sure he had ever seen on the faces of the people with whom he worked or drank.

It made him try to listen again to the things they were saying and singing. He thought about the words. And he was impressed. They were saying and singing things that expressed ambition, dynamism and a desire to get up and do something. But the ambitions expressed in these words were not about making money or getting promotion – they were about something quite different.

> *If you search for happiness you will not find it. But if you search for God you will find him – and you will get happiness thrown in.*
> C. S. Lewis (1898–1963)

> *Everybody wants to be happy.*
> Dan, *Beyond Borders* (Mandalay Films, 2003)

Andy really didn't know what to make of all this, and he wanted to find out more. He whispered to Julia, asking her how much longer the service would carry on.

'Don't worry,' she said, 'it will finish in just a moment – this is the last hymn.'

'Oh no!' he replied. 'Quick, now, let's get out.'

Julia knew far better than to argue with him, so she picked up her things and led him through the doors. As soon as they were outside Andy grabbed her by the hand and ran her quickly to the car. 'Get in,' he shouted. They

clambered in as fast as they could and he sped off away
from the church. Julia tried to catch her breath. But no
sooner had she got used to the fact that she was now in a
car racing along the road, than he had stopped and turned
off the engine.

'So what was all that about?' she said.

'All what?'

'All this dashing out and driving away.'

'Well, I just don't want Mum to see me, that's all.'

'Why ever not? She would be so pleased that you had
gone.'

'I know she would. But then she'd go on about it to me.
And she'd tell Dad, and he'd think that I wouldn't be on
his side any more. And . . . oh look, it's just too
complicated. I need space on my own to think it through.'

'OK, I can take a hint. I'll walk home from here,' Julia said.

'No,' he replied. 'No, don't take it that way. Please. It's
just that, if I'm going to think this out I've got to do it on
my own.'

*You have made us for yourself, and our hearts are restless
until they rest in you.*
                                    Augustine of Hippo (345–430)

*I'm always anxious, thinking I'm not living my life to the
fullest.*
                    Clementine, *Eternal Sunshine of the Spotless Mind*
                                          (Momentum Pictures, 2004)

'What can I do for you then?' asked the personnel officer
once Andy had sat down in front of her desk. 'Are you
after some more promotion already? I don't think we've
got any more opportunities at the . . .'

Andy interrupted her. 'No, it's nothing like that at all.'

'So what is it then?' she asked.

Andy paused for a moment and took in a deep breath. 'I want to have some time off.'

'I'm sorry, I'm not the person you need to see about holidays, you know that – you've been here long enough.'

'No, I know that. I'm not talking about a holiday. I want to have longer than that. I need to go away and think something through. Can I put everything on hold and take a long break away?'

This time it was her turn to breathe in deeply, as she raised her eyebrows and wondered what she should say.

'Is there some kind of problem here at work?'

'No, there's not. Well yes, there is. But it's not to do with work. It's to do with me. I just need some time away on my own, away from the pressure, away from the people, to think for myself.'

'I'm sorry,' she said, 'that's just not possible. We're running a business here, not a philosophy school. You can't just take time off when you want to do some thinking.'

'Then I'm afraid I'll have to leave,' said Andy.

'Pardon?'

'I said I'll have to leave. I'm handing in my notice right now.'

'Look,' she said, 'just hold on a minute. You've got a great career ahead of you here. Don't just throw it all away because you need to think about something. You'll lose everything – all that you've worked for.'

She did all that she could to persuade Andy to change his mind. But he wouldn't. He knew what he had to do, and nothing was going to stand in his way.

Word got around very quickly that he was leaving. People asked him where he was going and what he planned to do. But he didn't know how to answer those questions. Because even he didn't know where he was going or what he would do. All he knew was that he had to get away. He couldn't think it all through while he was working at that place – with the pressure, and the long hours, and the heavy drinking.

Over the next few days Andy sold his car and as much of his stuff as he could. He paid up the rent on his flat and cleared all his debts. It was then that he realised how much he must have spent in the time he had been in London. Sure, he'd earned a lot, but it had gone out as fast as it had come in – faster when he had taken out finance deals or hire-purchase.

Still, he had enough. So with cash in his pocket he went out to find the two things that he knew he must have – he bought a bicycle and a Bible.

He then loaded his rucksack with everything he had left, and took that, plus his bike, on a train back to his parents' house. Once there, he rummaged around in the loft until he found his old tent and a primus stove, which he strapped on to the bike.

Andy's mum and dad could not work out what he was doing. No matter how much they talked to him, he wouldn't say.

'Look,' he said, 'it's just something I've got to do.'

'But where are you going?' they asked.

'I don't know,' he replied. 'I'll head off down to the coast, but from there I really don't know.'

'Are you going abroad then?'

'Yeah, I expect so. I've got my passport, and I've got enough cash. Look, I'll be OK. Don't worry.'

With that he kissed his mum and shook his dad's hand. And then he was gone. Off down the road, and out of town.

He thought about calling in on Julia, but decided not to. He would be far better just going. So he went.

Despite all his drinking and his lack of exercise he was

still quite fit and strong. So he made good time as he headed south towards the coast. He followed the signs to Southampton, and then to the docks. From there he caught a ferry over to France.

Once he had arrived at the other side of the Channel he converted his money into francs and picked up a map. He sat for quite a while looking at it, wondering where he should go. It was then that he realised that it didn't really matter where he went. He wasn't there to see the country-side, he wasn't there as a tourist. He wasn't interested in sights and scenes or postcards and views. He was there to think and to read the Bible and to see if he could pray.

Among all my patients in the second half of life there has not been one whose problem in the last resort was not that of finding a religious outlook on life.

Carl Jung (1875–1961)

I believe in some kind of objective truth. We'll never get to see it, but the search for that is behind everything I do.

Daniel Beddingfield

*   *   *

It wasn't a very long train journey. But it was long enough to give Sharon time to think. And she didn't like that. Not when she was on her own, anyway.

She liked thinking when she was with Tony. Well, it was more like arguing actually. When they were in the Rising Sun with the others they would often drift over to a corner on their own where they would have a heated disagree-ment. It was never about themselves or personal issues. It was always about politics or economics. They argued about what the council should do on the estate or what the government should do for the country.

Sometimes they would stop and look at each other and laugh as they realised how bizarre this was. Here they were, in the pub with the biker gang who were getting steadily drunk or out of their heads on some tablets or other – and they were in the corner discussing politics. But that just seemed a natural thing to do with Tony. He wasn't like the others. Of course he got drunk, and he took whatever drugs he could get hold of. But there was also something different about him. Sharon couldn't really say what it was – but she liked it. She liked the way they talked and discussed and argued. She liked the way they could think together. Generally she just liked being with him.

Sure, he sometimes treated her roughly. All the gang saw their girls as their property, like an attachment to their bikes. So Tony would hit her, and knock her down, particularly if he was angry about something or was just in one of his moods. But Tony wasn't always like that. It was as if he just sometimes flipped into that kind of behaviour. He wasn't really like that. Not deep down. At heart he was kind and caring. He could be thoughtful. And Sharon liked thinking with him. What she didn't like was thinking on her own.

Perhaps that was why she took so readily to the drugs. She didn't take them to be sociable like some of the gang. In fact she didn't really take them very much at all when she was with others. Sharon used drugs when she was on her own. When there was no-one around to drown out her thoughts. When she needed a blanket to pull over her head.

Tony could get hold of any drugs she wanted. He always had lots of them. Sometimes he took a whole load himself. He was known in the gang as the guy who could take anything. That was something else that was puzzling about him. He didn't take drugs all the time – just occasionally. But, when he did, he really took them – he went on a binge, a complete bender. That was how he got his reputation. Sharon couldn't really make sense of it. It seemed as if Tony was two people in one. There was the kind, sensitive Tony who enjoyed being sober and thinking. Then there was the drunken, drugged-up Tony who just wanted to be out of it.

As the train came into the outskirts of London, Sharon too wanted to be out of it. She took out the small bottle of vodka she had bought on the estate just before she left – and used it to wash down the tablets Tony had given her that afternoon. Sharon felt the burning sensation as the drink passed down her throat – and she waited for the drugs to have their effect. She needed their effect. She needed it more that night than she ever had since Tony had first introduced her to them. She needed to feel what they could do for her. She needed to feel no feelings.

The train pulled into the station and the tannoy announced that this was the end of the line. But Sharon sat still. She watched the other passengers get up and leave. A businessman with a briefcase and an overnight bag. A young couple with their arms entwined around each other. A group of students jostling and joking together. Soon the train was quiet. Sharon was on her own. She took a deep breath, stood up, and walked towards the door as steadily as she could manage.

She was wearing a tight red dress with matching red shoes and a small jacket. In her handbag she carried the instructions the escort agency had given her. She was to hail a taxi and ask to be taken to the Strand Palace Hotel. There she should go to room 278 – in which she would find Dietmar and Helmut. They were German businessmen who were in London for a conference and fancied a bit of fun. They would take her out for dinner and then back to the hotel room where she was to entertain them in any way they wanted.

Sharon knew what that meant. She wasn't there just to be a pretty table decoration at dinner. She wasn't just there to play a role in the restaurant. She was their dessert. She was expected to play any role they wanted in the bedroom afterwards.

For a moment Sharon felt a little bit sick. Suddenly her mind drifted back several weeks to her first day at the studio. Once again she thought she might run, she might hide. But she didn't. She kept walking towards the taxi rank. Any feeling of fear or regret that might have begun to bubble up was soon smothered by the warm blanket of the vodka and the drugs.

They enabled her to feel strong and powerful; protected from the world by her narcotic shield; able to cope with anything.

And she did cope. She was everything that Dietmar and Helmut had hoped she would be. She played their games. She played her role. She fulfilled their fantasy. And it didn't feel like it hurt her, it didn't feel bad.

In fact she didn't feel anything – until she was sitting on the train on her way home. It was then that the drugs and the alcohol began to wear off and her feelings returned. It was then that she wanted her blanket once again – to smother her for ever, so that she would never wake up, and never have to feel anything again.

There is but one truly serious philosophical problem and that is suicide. Judging whether life is or is not worth living amounts to answering the fundamental question of philosophy.

Albert Camus (1913–1960)

There's things that gnaw at a man worse than dying.
Charlie Waite, *Open Range*
(Touchstone Pictures, 2003)

Sharon experienced that roller-coaster many times in the weeks and months that followed. The escort agency were very pleased with her. She knew how to act the parts that the clients wanted. She played many different roles for many different men.

And she could cope with it, as long as she had a bottle of vodka and some tablets to wrap herself up within. But when she came down, and thought about her life, she just wanted it all to be over.

She never spoke to Tony about those feelings, or the work that she was doing, for that matter. They both knew about it, of course. And they both knew that the other one knew. But it just wasn't something they talked about. It was their way of pretending that it was all OK, that it didn't matter, that it was just a job.

She wanted to talk to him. Many times she wanted to. But she didn't. There were other things they didn't talk about as well. Things that Tony wanted to tell her, but couldn't. About his parents, for instance. Except that, one day, he did.

10

'You're joking.'

'No, I'm not.'

'Come on, you are. You must be.'

Tony hesitated for a while. He seemed to be thinking about something. 'I tell you, I'm not,' he said eventually. 'My dad's a vicar.'

Sharon leant back against the wall and shook her head. They were out in the countryside in a spot to which they had been going quite often recently. It didn't take long to get there – especially with the way Tony drove his bike. But she liked it because it made them feel as if they were in another world, away from the estate, away from the modelling and the escort work, away from the gang and the Rising Sun, away from the drugs – well, most of them anyway; they usually took a joint or two with them.

This was a world of grass and trees, of nature and peace. They always sat in the same place, up against the same bit of wall, in the corner of the same field. But somehow it seemed different every time.

It was there that they would talk about themselves. And it was there that they would, sometimes, open up a chink in the armour and let down a bit of the wall.

That was what happened that day. For the first time Tony told her about his parents. He didn't see them very often. Not since he had left home. But sitting there, in the sunshine, with the cool breeze causing the tops of the tufts of grass to sway gently, for some reason he decided to bite the bullet and to tell Sharon about them.

It wasn't easy being the son of a vicar. It never had been. Other kids picked on him and teased him – whether it was in school or out on the street. Wherever he went, kids just seemed to assume that if his dad was so religious that he had taken it up as a job, and if Tony spent so much time in church, then he must be really soft.

Tony could remember the many days he came home with a cut lip or a bruised back – where he had been punched or kicked by some kid or other. He could remember the many nights when he lay in bed crying quietly to himself. He didn't tell his parents about it. He knew that would make it even worse. So he hid his pain, and his tears, as he cried all alone in the dark.

Looking back on it he wasn't quite sure when he made his decision. He was probably about thirteen or fourteen, maybe a bit younger. Anyway it was a real turning point in his life. He knew that he had a choice to make. He could carry on taking the insults and the beatings or he could do something about it. It was up to him.

It wasn't an easy decision to take. It hurt him. And it hurt his dad.

The fact was that Tony really liked his dad. He didn't just love him, with the blind love that all kids seem to have for their dads – whatever they are actually like. No, he really liked him as well. He enjoyed being with him. He was fascinated by the stories he told. The tales from the Bible always seemed to come alive when his dad told them. But there were other stories too. Stories from today, stories of the way in which God was so real to his dad, stories of miracles that his dad had seen – of prayers answered, of people's lives changed.

Tony hadn't just heard them from his dad, he had seen them for himself. And they had amazed him. Like, for instance, the time when Tony was eleven years old and needed a new bike. He always passed his bikes on to his younger brother, but there was no-one to hand one down to him. And his mum and dad didn't have enough money to buy him one. So they prayed. He would never forget that time. The whole family sat together round the large wooden table in the kitchen and prayed that God would provide a bike for Tony. It wasn't anything new to pray together round the table – they did it every day. But normally Tony was only half listening, and half joining in. However, that day he prayed with all the energy his little mind and body could muster. When his dad said, 'Father, if it is your will . . .' Tony prayed even harder in his mind, 'Yes, God, it is, it must be your will, please, please . . .'

As soon as they had finished praying Tony rushed to the front door to see if his new bike had been delivered. But it hadn't. It was then that his dad came and put his hand on his shoulder and suggested that they went out for a walk together. So they did. They walked for miles, out into the countryside, and they talked for hours. His dad told him about how he walked and talked with God day by day. He told him how he never needed to feel alone because he could know that God was always with him. He told him how he knew that he never needed to worry about anything because he could always trust the God who feeds the birds and clothes the flowers to feed and clothe him and his family.

But he also explained that God is not some magical slot machine in the sky who will pour out the jackpot for us whenever we pull the handle. He told Tony about really tough times he had experienced. About periods of pain and anguish, and times of doubt when he had felt that

God must be a million miles away if he exists at all. He told him how he had cried out to God, and not let go, and how eventually God had drawn him back into that close, intimate relationship once more.

Tony then turned to his dad and told him how he wanted to experience God as he did. He wanted to know what it was like to live closely with him, to walk with him and talk with him.

'Are you sure you don't just want God to give you that bike?'

'No,' said Tony, 'it's not that. I don't mind not having a bike. That's OK. I just want to know God like you do, Dad.'

His dad smiled and put his arm around Tony's shoulders. He would never forget that smile and that hug. Whatever happened in the years that followed, despite what he did and where he went, that smile and that hug were always as vivid and clear in Tony's memory every day as they were on that afternoon in the countryside.

Tony's dad looked down at his son and said, 'Why don't we pray now – and you can tell God what you have just told me.'

'Yeah,' said Tony.

So they sat together on the grass, leaning up against a wall, and there Tony prayed. 'God, I'm sorry that I just wanted the bike. What I really want is you. I know that if I got the bike it would be great and I'd love it. But I know I'd want something else, and then something else. What I really want, though, is you. I want to know you like Dad does. I want you to be with me all the time. I want you to never let me go. I want you to be my friend.'

Tony didn't see his dad crying. He just felt his gentle hug and warm kiss. But that wasn't all he felt. Deep down, inside, he could also feel another hug and another kiss.

That one wasn't physical and it wasn't from his dad. It seemed to be spiritual and it seemed to be from God.

Tony and his dad sat against that wall for a long time, talking together and praying together. His dad got out the little Bible that he always carried with him and they read some passages together.

> *Blessed are the poor in spirit, for theirs is the kingdom of heaven.*
> *Blessed are those who mourn, for they will be comforted.*
> *Blessed are the meek, for they will inherit the earth.*
> *Blessed are those who hunger and thirst for righteousness, for they will be filled.*
> *Blessed are the merciful, for they will be shown mercy.*
> *Blessed are the pure in heart, for they will see God.*
> *Blessed are the peacemakers, for they will be called sons of God.*
> *Blessed are those who are persecuted because of righteousness, for theirs is the kingdom of heaven.*
>
> Jesus Christ (Matthew 5:3–10)

It was getting dark when they eventually stood up and it was pitch-black and cold when they finally arrived back at the vicarage. But in Tony's mind a light was beginning to shine, and his heart was strangely warm.

Very often Tony wished that he could go back to that wall to be with his dad and with God. He wished it when the other kids at school started teasing him. He wished it when they started bullying him. He particularly wished it on the day when four of them set on him and beat him up really bad. But he never could get back there.

Something had happened. Tony didn't know what it was. But for some reason his dad had become very busy in his work. There was some project or other that his dad had been asked to organise, and it seemed to take over his life. The phone was always ringing and he was hardly ever at home. He used to come in to Tony's room at night and say how sorry he was that they hadn't had any time together that day. But Tony didn't want to hear that. He just kept his head down under the covers and pretended that he was asleep. So that his dad wouldn't see his tears or hear his cries.

As he lost touch with his dad, so he also lost touch with God. It didn't happen overnight. It was a gradual process. But it ended with his decision – he made a definite choice.

Tony had tried to cope as long as he could. But in the end he couldn't stand it any more. He had decided that he would have to show the other kids that he wasn't really soft. He had to play the part that they wanted. He had to take on the role that they required.

First he started swearing. Not very much at first, just occasional words. But, in time, his repertoire grew and his language became as rough and profane as any of them. Then he started hanging out at night with the other kids. His mum and dad gave him a curfew, but he always stayed out beyond that. Then they banned him from going out at all – but he escaped out of the back door or window. That was the time when he started smoking. He didn't like it at all at first. The cigarettes tasted like stale cheese, they made his mouth feel burnt and dry – and they made his stomach feel queasy. For quite a while he would light a cigarette but not smoke it very much. Instead he held it in his hand – always positioning it in such a way that the smoke rose up over his fingers and stained them yellow, like a regular smoker, like the others in the gang.

It was a long time before he eventually got used to the cigarettes. And by then his friends had started using drugs. So he didn't delay. He got stuck into those straight away. In fact he took to the drugs with such enthusiasm that the dealers soon chose him to take the risks of supplying them to the others. He was very happy to do that – not least because it gave him enough money to indulge in as many drugs as he wanted for himself – and he was able to save up to buy a second-hand motorbike.

Tony's mum and dad had no idea where he was getting his money from. And they certainly didn't approve of his motorbike.

'We're only worried that you're going to have an accident and get hurt one day,' said his mum.

'Yes, it's just because we love you, son,' added his dad.

'No you don't. You don't care about me at all. You never have. You never will.' Tony shouted those words at his parents. He didn't believe them. He knew they weren't true in the slightest. He just used them because he knew it would hurt his mum and dad. He meant to hurt them. He meant for them to feel pain. He wanted them to feel what he felt.

That was why he moved out. He did it in the course of an argument. He was shouting and swearing at them, when suddenly he grabbed his coat, pulled on his boots and roared off on his motorbike. That was it. He was gone. And he had no intention of going back again – no matter how much he really wanted to.

For a while he dossed down on other people's floors. But then he met some guys from the big estate a few miles away. They were in a motorbike gang, and he found that he was able to play the role and act the part that enabled him to fit in. So they became mates, and he moved in with some of them. It wasn't long after that that he met Sharon. And it wasn't much longer before they started going out with each other. But it was a long time before he took the risk of telling her that his dad was a vicar.

'You're joking,' she had said.

'No, I'm not,' he had replied.

'Come on, you are. You must be.'

It was then that he thought perhaps he would pretend that he was joking actually. He thought deeply about it for a few moments. Did he really want to admit it to her? Eventually he had replied, 'I tell you, I'm not. My dad is a vicar.'

Sharon took quite a while to recover from that bit of news. All she could do was to sit there and shake her head. But when she eventually got her mind around it she suddenly jumped up, roughly brushed the dirt off the seat of her jeans and said, 'Hey, let's go and visit him.'

'Now you're joking,' said Tony.

'No, I'm not,' replied Sharon. 'I've never been inside a vicarage before. Come on, it will be fun. We can have a laugh.'

'I can't do that. I haven't been home at all since I left – and that was ages ago.'

It took a long time and quite a few joints before Tony finally agreed to take Sharon to visit his parents. And it was only as he was starting up the bike that she told him that she wanted to go home and get changed first.

'But look,' he said, 'it's only just down the road from here. If you want to get changed first we'll have to go all the way home and then all the way out here again.'

'I know,' replied Sharon, 'but I want to wear something different to meet your mum and dad.'

So they did go home. And Sharon did change her clothes. She certainly wore something different. She put on the shortest, tightest skirt she had, and stockings underneath – with the tops showing below her hem. She hunted until she found her almost transparent red blouse. It was in the pile in the corner ready for the next trip to the launderette, but she straightened it out and stretched it over her breasts. Finally she covered her face in make-up before pulling on her black leather jacket and red high-heeled shoes – and climbing on to the back of Tony's motorbike.

'If a vicar's son brings a prostitute home to the vicarage then at least she should look like one,' Sharon said to Tony as they roared off up the road. He didn't reply. They hadn't really talked openly with each other about Sharon's escort work. And it didn't seem a good time to start now.

In the months that followed, Sharon thought many times about that afternoon. She had deliberately set out to shock Tony's mum and dad. She was determined to provoke them. She expected them to be disgusted with her. She assumed that they were bound to reject her.

Only Tony's mum and dad didn't. They obviously heard his motorbike arrive and they were at the door waiting to greet him before he had even put it up on its stand. And that was when they saw her. They looked shocked, but they immediately came out and welcomed her into their home. Sharon acted like a tart, she played the role perfectly, but all the time Tony's parents treated her with love and respect. They sat her on their newest chair, they brought tea to her and served it on their finest china. They brought out the family albums and showed her photographs of Tony as a little boy. When Tony's brother arrived home they introduced her to him as 'Sharon, our Tony's girlfriend.'

Sharon didn't know what to make of this. She was puzzled – in much the same way that she was with Tony himself sometimes. There was something about them all that was different. She didn't know what it was. She couldn't even begin to understand it. But she liked it. She found herself strangely attracted to this home and the family that lived in it.

And that worried her. How could she be attracted to a vicar and his wife? Why did she want to be with them? What right had she got to be there?

The questions grew to a crescendo in her mind. They drowned out the conversation in the room. It was too much. She couldn't take it any longer. She had to get out. Without warning, Sharon suddenly stood up and exclaimed, 'Come on, Tony, I've had enough of this place. It's boring here. Let's go down the pub.'

Tony was surprised by her sudden outburst. But he was more than willing to go along with her. Because he too was finding that his heart was being torn apart within him. And he didn't know how to cope with it. He wanted to fall on to the floor and grab hold of his dad's feet. He wanted to say sorry for what he had done, for how he had treated them. And he wanted to take his mum in his arms and hug her more than he ever had before. But he couldn't bring himself to do it, any of it, not in front of Sharon anyway – never, not ever.

So, as soon as Sharon headed towards the door, Tony immediately followed her. They moved so quickly that they left his mum and dad behind in the room. Grabbing their coats they almost ran to the bike, which started first time and sent a spray of gravel into the air as it took off. It was only as they turned out of the drive and on to the road that Sharon looked back. She saw that Tony's mum and dad had come out to the doorway, and were standing arm in arm, warmly waving to their drug-dealing son and his prostitute girlfriend.

Tony and Sharon didn't talk about the events of that afternoon. But they both thought about them many times. It played on their minds. And it tugged at their hearts.

Love is the secret of life. Someone who hasn't learned to love hasn't begun to live. That is life.
Catherine Bramwell-Booth (1883–1987)

The greatest thing you'll ever learn is just to love and be loved in return.
Christian, *Moulin Rouge*
(Twentieth Century Fox Entertainment, 2001)

The months that followed were a period of personal internal turmoil for both of them. It was a time when they needed their drugs more than ever. Tony increased his dealing and Sharon took more escort bookings, as well as some very well-paid but rather painful photo-shoots. This gave them enough money to have any drugs they wanted, morning, noon or night. They smoked them, they swallowed them, they snorted them. They did anything they could to smother themselves with their narcotics.

But drugs never last. No-one can stay high for ever. Even a binge has to come to an end at some time. And it was then that they both began to wonder if there could be another way to live.

'If only we could start all over again. If only we could get away from our lives, away from the drugs, away from the modelling and the prostitution. Then we would be free. Then we would . . .' So many times the same train of thought went through their minds. They didn't talk to each other about it. They couldn't. Until one day Tony found a way to raise the subject with Sharon – a subject that she herself had been wanting to talk about all the time.

'What do you think about Australia?' he said.

'Pardon?'

'I said what do you think about Australia? How would you fancy us moving out there?'

'Why?' she asked.

'Isn't it obvious? To get away from this estate and the drugs and my dealing and your modelling. Sharon, we could start again. We could be free. Let's leave the drugs behind and start a new life out there.'

Sharon looked at his face. Suddenly he looked like an eleven-year-old. He looked like he had in the photos his mum had shown her. He looked keen, enthusiastic and vulnerable.

'Tony – that's the best thing you've said.'

'So you'd like to go?'

'Of course I would. I just want to get away. I want to start again.'

Tony took her in his arms with that tenderness that she only knew from him sometimes, when it seemed to seep through the hard act he was playing. For a while they simply sat there, leaning against the wall, holding each other.

Eventually Sharon broke the silence. 'Why Australia?' she said.

'You've seen the adverts. "In Australia you can . . ." they say. It's a land of opportunity. They want people to go there. They want people to come. You don't even have to have a criminal record any more.'

They laughed together with a lightness and happiness that neither of them had known for a long time.

Almost immediately Sharon stopped the modelling and the escort work. And it seemed as if a huge weight had been taken off her shoulders. Tony even stopped his dealing, and both of them cut right back on the amount of drugs they used themselves.

For several days they became like little children who look forward to Christmas or birthdays with an excitement that they can't contain. They visited the library and looked at books, they went to the travel agents and bought their tickets. That took most of the money that they possessed. Tony had to sell his bike and his stash of drugs. Sharon calculated that once they had paid all that they had to in order to get out there, they would have enough money to rent a room somewhere and to live for a few weeks. 'By then we'll have got jobs, both of us,' she said to Tony.

They even decided to get married. 'Why not?' they thought. It's all part of starting again, beginning over. It wasn't a big wedding. Not many people came. But it was a good excuse to drink up the last of their drink and to swallow, smoke or snort the rest of their drugs. For the last few days and nights they hardly stopped, nor did the others who had come to help them to celebrate their wedding, to finish off their drink and drugs, and to wave goodbye as they set off to the airport.

The main thing I have always asked from life is freedom.
Outer and inner freedom.

Somerset Maugham (1874–1965)

11

Victor Frankel was a Jew who survived the concentration camps of the Second World War. Afterwards he reflected upon the question why some prisoners managed to keep going, whereas others gave up and died. He believed that it wasn't really to do with their physical strength, but rather their sense of purpose and meaning in life. In his book Man's Search for Meaning he wrote, 'The prisoner who had lost his faith in his own future was doomed. With his loss of belief in the future, he also lost his spiritual hold; he let himself decline and became subject to mental and physical decay.' However, if you know where you are going and what you are living for, then, no matter how bad life may become, you can keep going.

I was looking at some kids the other day. I watched them play together. They argued and fought. 'I hate you,' one said. 'I hate you even more,' replied the other. You might think that nothing could ever bring them back together again – that their relationship would be broken for ever. But it isn't like that. Very soon they've forgotten about what they said or did. And they are all over each other – they're the best of friends again. It's as if the argument never happened.

Well, that's a bit like it was with Jenny. I didn't go any further down that path towards the Maths block. I turned and walked away. I didn't let them know that I had heard what they had said.

Of course I cried that night, mourning for the feelings of security and stability that I had lost. But I did everything I could to put things right with my old friends. I stopped borrowing money from them. From that day onwards I never asked them for any money. I sat down with a piece of paper and calculated how much I owed them all, and how long it would take to pay it back. That worried me a bit so I asked at the post office if I could work longer hours. They said that I could, and I was able to earn enough to clear all my debts over the next four months.

It was then that Jenny asked me if I would like to go on a camp with her. I didn't quite know what she was talking about first of all. But it seemed that she and her family went to the local church on a Sunday and the youth group were going to go to Exmoor for a week.

I didn't know any of the other young people who were going – even the ones that Jenny told me about; they were all in other years at school and we didn't have much to do with them. Anyway, the fact was that I knew Jenny and she wanted me to go on the camp with her – so that was good enough for me.

I asked my mum and dad and they said that it was fine by them. They never went to the church, in fact I can't remember a single time when they went to any church, but they were happy for me to go if I wanted. So I did.

The camp wasn't quite what I had expected. I thought that we would spend most of our time going off on our own and messing around in the woods – getting lost and things. But we actually spent a lot of time sitting in a big tent listening to the curate from the church talking to us about God. This totally bored me, and I wondered why on earth I had agreed to come with Jenny.

Of course we did go out sometimes. And we did get lost a few times – particularly when we went on that crazy night hike organised by the boys in the group. Obviously the curate was more keen to develop their sense of self-assurance than he was to get us all back to the camp in time to get some sleep. So, even when they clearly didn't have the faintest idea where we were and they were just guessing a direction for us, he accepted what they said and told them how impressed he was with their confidence.

He wasn't quite so impressed when we ended up in a stream, and we found that we had been heading in the wrong direction for the past hour. But still, he didn't want to criticise. I was really surprised by that. I expected him to go right off the deep end, and shout at them. But he didn't. It was then that I began to wonder why this man was like this. What made him behave in the way that he did? And the others too – some of the other members of the youth group who were into all this stuff about God, they really seemed to have something different about them.

So, when we were next in the big tent, I started listening to the curate instead of ignoring him and drifting off into a day-dream.

Then, the more I listened, the more interested I became. Something happened to me that week in that camp. At the time I wasn't really sure what it was. As the curate spoke each day, I found that the things he said began to make sense. He told us about God, and how he created us to live in a relationship with him. He explained how everything had gone wrong in the world because we had chosen to reject God and to go our own way. He then told us how Jesus had come to provide a way for us to be forgiven, so that we can come back into a relationship with him.

It was when he talked about a relationship with God that I particularly paid attention. Although my parents are not Christians and have never been to church, I myself had never really doubted that God existed – I always assumed that he was there, I just wasn't sure how I could make contact with him, or if I really wanted to.

Anyway, the curate's talks helped me to see how that was possible. I began to understand why Jesus had died on a cross. I'd never understood that before. I'd learned about it at school, of course, but I'd always picked up the idea that it was some kind of mistake. I assumed that Jesus had not intended to die – his life had all just gone horribly wrong and ended in this disastrous death. The curate helped me to see that Jesus had said that he had come to die; that was his plan, he intended to lay down his life. I must say it took me a long time to grasp that one. I just couldn't see what the point was of that.

It was only when the curate told one of his little stories that it began to make sense. He asked us to imagine that he had been caught speeding in his car. Well, that was not very likely but we played along with him and tried to imagine it. 'OK then,' he said, 'now imagine that when I get to the court I find that the judge is my favourite uncle.' I was with him so far, but couldn't for the life of me see what this had to do with Jesus. 'Now, my uncle,' he continued, 'loves me and wants the very best for me. But he is also completely fair and just – he won't do any shady business or any crooked deals, he's completely straight. So what can he do? He can't just let me off, no matter how much he might want to. If he did then he wouldn't be standing up for truth and justice. He'd have become crooked and bent.'

At this point the curate hesitated to let us think about the judge's predicament. I couldn't see any way in which the judge could stand up for justice and yet also be loving to his nephew at the same time. And I still couldn't figure out whatever this had to do with Jesus.

Then he continued: 'So, if the judge is to be just and fair he must fine me the proper fine for that offence – let's suppose it's £1,000. I might then be shocked that my uncle could give me a fine like that. "OK, you've stood up for truth and justice," I might say to him, "but where's mercy, where's love? I thought you cared about me, I thought you wanted the best for me."

'Well,' the curate continued, 'then imagine that my uncle, the judge, got out of his seat, came over to me, took out his own cheque-book and wrote a cheque for £1,000. You see, by paying the fine himself he has brought together justice and love. He has done something which is just and loving at the same time. He has kept the law but also enabled me to go free.

'And that is what God did when he sent Jesus to die on the cross. He provided a way for all of the wrong things we have ever done, to be paid for not by ourselves but by God himself. He couldn't have just let us off for the wrong things we have done – if he had done that then nothing would ever matter again. When Jesus hung on that cross he was saying, "Sin matters, everything you've ever done wrong really matters, but I will take the penalty for you, so that you can be forgiven, so that you can go free, so you can start a new life in a relationship with God."'

As the curate said those words it all clicked into place in my mind. I could understand it – it made sense.

He then finished his talk by asking us all if we were prepared to 'take God's cheque'. Would we receive the forgiveness that Jesus offers us, and start out on a new life in a relationship with God? He explained that this would mean many changes in our lives. 'Relationships mean change,' he said, 'you know that. If you start going out with a new boyfriend or girlfriend you don't stay the same, do you? You change. And it's like that with God. If you come into a relationship with him then many things will change in your life – and you need to say that you are willing to change in any way that he asks you.'

At that point it seemed that a number of the kids on the camp didn't want to hear any more. Some started shuffling, a few made an excuse to go out to the toilet. But others of us, myself included, stayed riveted to the spot. We wanted to know what we had to do to accept this cheque, to come into this relationship with God.

'I tell you what I'll do,' the curate said. 'I'm going to pray a prayer now, and you can pray it as well if you want to. Let me tell you what I am going to pray in my prayer – so you can see if you want to be in on it or not. I'm going to pray, "God, I'm sorry for all the wrong I've done; please forgive me. Thank you that Jesus died so that I can be forgiven. Right now I give my whole life to you. From now on I want to follow you and serve you whatever the cost. Please come and live inside me, please cleanse me, please enable me to live for you." Now, if you want to pray that prayer, if you really mean it, then just say it along with me as I pray it.'

I can't really tell you what happened at that point. All I can say is that I prayed that prayer along with him. And it seemed to me that, from that time on, God came to be with me. I felt as if the doors of heaven opened, as if I could now speak to God any time I wanted, and as if he would speak to me.

It was a turning point in my life. I knew that, from then on, God would always be with me. And he was. Of course I drifted away from him many times. But he always seemed to pull me back. And I knew, from that time on, that God would never leave me.

It made it so much easier to cope with the situation at home. As I lay in bed and listened to the crashing down below, I didn't feel alone or helpless. I knew that God was with me. And so I would snuggle down in my bed and pray.

You might expect me to say that I prayed for my dad and he completely changed – giving up the alcohol and becoming a Christian himself. Well, that didn't happen. Sure, I prayed for him. But for some reason God has not answered that prayer – yet. Life was still tough. In fact, it was going to get much tougher in the years ahead.

*   *   *

They sat in the airport lounge for what seemed like a lifetime. They lost count of the number of times that the tannoy told them the plane was going to be delayed. Tony lay across a row of seats and drifted off into a fitful sleep. But Sharon just sat and picked away at the fraying hole at the side of her bag. When she had pulled at it so much she was afraid that it was all going to fall apart in her hands, she quickly put it down and looked for something else to distract her.

'One of those books,' she suddenly said to herself. 'That's it, I'll buy a book.'

She hadn't really read anything for ages – apart from the odd newspaper or magazine. So she didn't know where to start looking around the well-stocked bookshop. Most just looked too big or too boring. She was going to give up looking when she saw the section labelled 'Romance'. She pulled out a book, read through the blurb, and put it back on the shelf. She did it again with another book, and another, and another. It wasn't that she couldn't find one that she wanted to read. The fact was that she wanted to read all of them. She wanted to find out what happened to the characters whose pictures she saw on the front. She wanted to join them in their lives.

Eventually Sharon decided on one. She paid the young girl at the till and tucked the book into her bag, where it poked out slightly through the frayed hole.

British Airways Flight 307 to Sydney, Australia, took off about two hours late. Within minutes of leaving the ground Tony was fast asleep and Sharon tried to follow him.

Some while later, when she still couldn't drift off, she reached up for her bag and pulled out her new book. She wasn't a fast reader, but it was only a little book and it was a long flight. It was long enough for her to read every page. It was long enough for her to get to know every character. And it was long enough for her to wish that she could feel what they felt. To her it seemed as if she was some kind of alien looking in on a strange planet – she could see a world in which the people had emotions and feelings about which she knew nothing.

Sharon turned over the last page and then laid the book down in her lap. She closed her eyes and thought about herself. In particular she thought about her heart, and how hard she had become. Her mind flicked back to the moments of happiness and friendship and love she had known occasionally when she was a child. She tried to relive some of the emotions and feelings that she must have experienced at those times. But it was no good. It didn't work. Sharon took a deep breath and let it out slowly through her nostrils. How she longed to be soft again. How she longed to feel once more.

'Drinks?'

'Sorry, what?'

'Would you like a drink?' the stewardess said.

'Um . . . Yeah, yes I do,' Sharon replied. 'Give me a double vodka, will you?'

> *All this time I've been packing ice around my heart. How do I make it melt?*
> Ada Monroe, *Cold Mountain* (Miramax Films, 2003)

They can always spot them – anywhere. *Why is that?* Sharon questioned herself, but had no answer. *Wherever you go in the world, druggies can always spot druggies.*

She and Tony had done everything they could to stay out of the drugs scene since they had arrived in Sydney. They had found somewhere to live, bought some food, and spent every hour they could looking for work. No matter how hard they tried they couldn't find what they wanted. But wherever they went they did find what they didn't want – people who dealt or smoked or swallowed or snorted.

Tony and Sharon found what so many others had discovered before them – that no matter how far you run away you can't run away from yourself, you always take yourself with you.

And they had taken their craving for drugs with them. It was a craving that they couldn't resist, no matter how much they tried.

When they bought their first bit of cannabis they knew it would not be their last. And they knew that this would mean that their money would run out very fast indeed. They tried to ration themselves, but they couldn't. They didn't write anything down, they didn't need to; they knew that the money would very soon be gone.

It was then that Tony showed Sharon the advert in the paper. He'd been buying the local rag each day and poring over the job adverts. But this time he had found one for Sharon.

'I think you should do that.' That was all he said as he passed her the page with the big circle pencilled on it.

'Girls wanted,' the advert said, 'by massage parlour. Must be willing to give a full service to any client. Experience preferred but not essential.'

Sharon didn't read any further. She dropped the paper down on to the floor and looked at her husband. Her mind raced back over the past few days. The wedding, the vows, the promises, the new life, the new home, the new beginning.

'I think you should do that.' Tony said again. 'We've got to do something. What else are we going to do?'

It was several hours before Sharon could bring herself to pick up that paper again. By then Tony had gone out and she was on her own. She tore out the advert and stuffed it into her pocket before opening the door and walking out into the street.

The map had shown her that it wasn't very far at all from where they were living to the massage parlour. She decided to walk, thinking that then she could always turn round again and go home. But she didn't. She didn't even take any detours or double back on herself. She walked directly there, went up to the door and went straight in.

There didn't seem to be any formal interviewing process. The woman who ran the place simply looked her up and down and asked her if she had any experience in this line of work.

Sharon told her about her modelling and escort work.

'Well it won't be like that here, you know. No nice studios or fancy meals and posh cars. It's "Wham Bam Thankyou Ma'am" here. But you've got to give them what they want – whatever it is, and whoever they are. Do you understand?'

'Yes,' Sharon replied. She understood. She understood only too well.

A young girl called Tracy was told to show her around, which she did, explaining how the system worked.

'If she likes you and she thinks you're good for business she'll put you out here,' Tracy said, pointing to the lounge area. It contained a collection of old and rather grubby armchairs and sofas. Nothing matched or looked terribly comfortable. There was a bar at the end of the room and a music system in the corner.

'This is the best place to be. I'm in here all the time,' she continued. ' 'Cos here you're much more likely to get some business. If you can get them to sit down with you on one of these seats then they might choose you. But you won't be in here for a long time, I can tell you.'

'So where will I be?' asked Sharon.

'Over there, in the line-up,' Tracy replied. She pointed to a space that ran along the long wall of the room, in the direction that most of the chairs were facing. 'You'll be told when to come in, with all the others, and you'll have a number in your hand. Then you stand there until the ones they want have been chosen. If you're lucky, one of them will call your number. If not, you walk back out of the way with the others.'

In the days that followed, Sharon stood in that line-up many times. She never once knew what she really wanted to happen as she waited there. Whatever happened she always wished that it had been the opposite.

If her number was not called, then she worried about what Tony would say if she went home without any money from the night.

On the other hand, if her number was called, then she immediately wished that it hadn't been. Now she had to go with this man and do whatever he wanted. Whether he was clean or dirty, whether he was eighteen or eighty, still she had to go with him – and she had to pretend that she was really keen to do it.

Most nights her number would be called several times. And at the end she would go home in a taxi, paying the driver with a note taken off the pile of cash in her hand. When she got in, Tony would nearly always be asleep. He didn't wake as she got undressed and slipped into bed beside him. He didn't see how she put the pile of money on her bedside table and how she lay awake looking at it. He didn't know that she just lay there and stared at it. She felt unable to move, unable to get away, unable to escape. She felt paralysed and powerless.

Even in the morning Sharon never touched the money. She didn't want to have anything to do with it. She just left it there until he picked it up.

12

Ludwig Wittgenstein, a great philosopher, told a story of a man who was desperately trying to escape from a house. He tried the window but it wouldn't budge, he tried to break the glass but it was too thick. He looked up the chimney but it was too small. He even attempted to get through the panel that lead to a secret passageway, but that was blocked. Finally, he collapsed on a chair in total despair. There was no answer, there was no way he could ever get out of this place. Then he noticed something out of the corner of his eye. The door had been open all the time.

Day after day, Andy cycled and read and camped and read some more. Sometimes he sat in the sunshine by the side of the road with the Bible out on his lap. Other times he stayed up most of the night reading in his tiny tent by the light of his cycle torch.

He remembered, from one of his long conversations with Julia, how she had told him that if he was ever to read the Bible it would be best for him to start with the New Testament. So he did. He began with Matthew's gospel, chapter 1. It very nearly ended there, too, because it was a long list of names. How was that going to help him to find the answer to his search? If he had been reading it at home he may well have put it down at that point and gone off to the pub.

But he wasn't at home. He was miles from home. And he was there because he wanted answers. He had come too far, and burned too many bridges, to turn back now. So he pressed on. He soon found he was reading about the life of Jesus, the things he did and the things he said. He didn't quite know what to make of them. Did he believe them? Did they really happen? How could he know?

Sometimes, he found himself praying as he read. They weren't long complicated prayers. He wasn't even sure if they were proper prayers at all. He was just calling out to God in his mind, saying, *If you really are there, then I want to come to know you.* Or, *If the Bible really is important, please help me to understand it.* Or sometimes just *Help me God, help me.*

If Julia had been with him she would have told him that those were real prayers. In fact they were the best kind of prayers that anyone could pray. But Julia wasn't there. He was on his own. And that was the way he had wanted it to be.

Over the days that followed he travelled many miles. He cycled along little lanes past farmhouses with their big wide fields. He stopped in small villages where he bought sticks of bread and lumps of cheese. Occasionally he bought some wine to go with it. But he didn't get drunk. He wanted a clear head to think and to pray.

Sometimes he met people who could speak English, either in the villages or in a campsite. Occasionally he joined with them for meals, or they even cycled some of the same route together. But most of the time Andy was on his own. He often felt lonely. Many times he thought of packing it all in and going back to England. If he went back to his work quickly he might even get his old job back. Or if he didn't, he could find another.

But those ideas never lasted long. Even if he thought like that for a whole day, and went to bed determined to set off for home in the morning, when he woke up and saw the sun rising over the trees, and heard the birds singing, he changed his mind. 'If there is a God who created all this – then I want to find him,' he said to himself.

One afternoon, after three weeks in France, he lay back beside his tent – resting the Bible on his chest. It was open at the very last page. He had read it all – the whole New Testament. All the way from Matthew to Revelation – he had gone through every page and read every word. But still he had not found God. He didn't quite know what to do. For a moment he lay there looking up at the sky, with the few wisps of cloud and the occasional bird. Was this the end? Was it now all over for him? He had read all that Julia had suggested – and nothing had happened. Perhaps there was no God. Perhaps it was all just a load of old fairy-tales.

Andy grabbed hold of the Bible and held it up in front of his face. He lay still, staring at it. Had it all been for nothing? Was it all just a waste of time? He began to think of the things he had given up in order to read that book – the money, the car, the girls, the drink. Anger welled up from deep within him. If he'd had anyone there to shout at he would have shouted at them. If he thought that God existed he would have screamed at him. But what was the point? He'd only be shouting at the sky.

Suddenly he jumped up and threw the Bible into the corner of his tent. He didn't care where it landed. He didn't care if he ever found it again.

Andy picked up his bike and jumped on. He cycled out of the campsite and along the lane to the town nearby where there was a supermarket that sold beer. He bought a crate of French lager and balanced it precariously on the handlebars as he cycled back to the camp. Once he got there he called to some of the other lads on the site and invited them to join him for a beer or two. They brought some cans over, and some wine. One of them even had some spirits of some sort – it was a bit rough but it was alcohol, and so they drank it.

Some of them could speak English and they talked together about their experiences of travelling around France.

'Have you been down south yet, Andy?' one said.

'No – why?'

'You know, you can have a great time down there – with all the festivals and everything.'

'Well, I don't think I want to cycle that far really. I'm thinking of going home.' Even as he said it, he thought how pathetic he sounded.

'You don't want to go home if you don't have to. I tell you, if I was you I'd get down to the festivals tomorrow. There's a train station up the road. If you've got the money you can travel down in style.'

'I don't know – anyway, pass me another lager, will you?'

When Andy crawled into his tent that night he was well and truly plastered – as drunk as he ever had been when he was in London. He practically passed out on the floor and lay there for hours. He didn't really get up the next day, except to clean himself up a bit and buy some bread. He drank some more that night, but there wasn't very much for him this time, just a bottle of lager that somehow got left behind, and some cheap wine that he bought from the camp shop.

It was when he woke up the following morning that he decided that he would do something. He took down his tent, packed it away, and cycled to the train station. It took him a while to figure out the train system and timetables, but he was able to plan a route down to the south. In order to get on the main train he had a number of smaller journeys to do first – and a lot of time sitting on benches in railway stations.

It was while he was sitting in one station that his mind went back to his visit to Julia's church. He thought about the people he had seen there – and their expressions, their joy, their peace. Could it really all be one big fairy-tale? Had they simply believed a fantasy? Or could it be that, for some reason, there was something blocking him from meeting with God in the way that they had?

Andy struggled with his thoughts, not sure what to do. Finally he decided that he was going to search again. He dug around in the corner of his rucksack and pulled out his Bible. When he had packed up at the campsite he had thought about throwing it away, but he knew that he couldn't do that. So he had chucked it in his bag with all his other things. And now he was glad that it was still there.

He decided that he would start again at the beginning of the New Testament and read through to the end. But this time he would pray, really pray, that if there was something that was standing in the way of him meeting with God, then it would go.

The next day Andy was on his own in a carriage on a train heading south. He was reading his Bible and had reached the passage in Luke's gospel which told the story of a prostitute who came to Jesus. She had stood behind Jesus and wept, so that her tears fell over his feet. The people who were there at the time tried to reject her, but Jesus accepted her and told her, 'Your sins are forgiven.'

As Andy read those words he began to cry. First small

tears trickled out slowly from the corner of his eyes, then bigger drops, turning into floods which poured down his cheeks.

As he read and re-read those words of Jesus he realised that he was just like that prostitute. Of course he wasn't on the game; he didn't stand on street corners or go to hotels. But he had sold his body just the same. He had a life, with abilities and talents. But what had he done with it? He had sold it for money. Anything for money.

Geoff was right, everyone had a price. He had accepted a bribe. He had believed that nothing was worth more than money. He thought back to his time at work, the things he did, the ways in which he treated people. He remembered how he would do anything for money – as long as the price was right.

Andy felt just like that prostitute, and now he was crying at Jesus' feet. Was this the first time in his life that Andy had admitted that he had got it all wrong? Perhaps it was. The arrogant, self-opinionated, success-driven Andy was crying at Jesus' feet asking for forgiveness for the way in which he had led his life.

It was at that point that the guard appeared. He had been watching Andy from a distance and he had now come to check up on him. Unfortunately he didn't speak English and Andy couldn't understand his French, so communication was a bit difficult between them. But it seemed that the guard was just concerned that Andy might be thinking of committing suicide – and he didn't want that happening on his train.

Andy managed to tell him that suicide was the last thing on his mind at that moment, and that he was perfectly alright really. He showed him his Bible and the guard nodded and turned away with one of those expressions that said it all – 'religious nutcase'.

As the guard left him, the train pulled in to the station at Avignon. Andy decided that he would get out at this point and find somewhere to camp. He collected his bike from the train and loaded on his tent and equipment. A few minutes later he was heading south looking for a campsite. He soon came across a small village with a campsite near a church. He had just finished pitching his tent when the church bells started ringing. Andy sat and listened to them for a while, before grabbing his Bible and running across to the church.

Once he got there he carefully opened the door and walked in quietly. He sat down on a pew at the back. When the service began he didn't understand any of it. Not a thing. But he was aware of a sense of peace and of God's presence. In fact the more he thought about it, the more he could sense God in that place.

As the service continued Andy knelt down, on his own, and prayed. It wasn't a fancy prayer, but he meant it. He said sorry to God for the way in which he had used his life. He said sorry for selling himself to the highest bidder. He told God that he now wanted a different ambition, he wanted to live for others not for himself, he wanted to make a difference in the world, not just to make money. He wanted to change. He wanted to be different. He asked God to change him, to make him different. He asked Jesus to come into his life and to enable him to begin again.

He didn't cry like he had on the train. In fact, the others in the church who looked round at him wouldn't have thought that anything special was happening at all. But he knew. He was aware of it. Andy knew that he had been forgiven, in the same way that the prostitute had. He knew that he had now started again, with God right in the centre of his life. He knew that from now on he had new hopes, new dreams, new ambitions.

As he walked out of the church he felt as if he was bouncing along on cushions of air. He was so excited that he wanted to tell someone – anyone. But who could he tell, out here on his own, in a small French village? Who would speak to him? Who would understand him?

He walked back towards the campsite – and as he passed through the gates he saw a Moroccan man who was putting up a tent. Andy smiled at him and said, 'Hello'. The man immediately stood up and began speaking to him in fluent English. It was then that he noticed Andy's Bible and said, 'Ah, I see that you are a religious man.'

With confidence and assurance in his voice, Andy replied, 'I am a Christian.'

If you confess with your mouth, 'Jesus is Lord,' and believe in your heart that God raised him from the dead, you will be saved. For it is with your heart that you believe and are justified, and it is with your mouth that you confess and are saved. As the Scripture says, 'Everyone who trusts in him will never be put to shame.'

St Paul (Romans 10:9–11)

When I die don't build a monument to me. Don't bestow on me degrees from great universities. Just say I tried to clothe the naked. Say that I tried to house the homeless. Let people say I tried to feed the hungry.

Martin Luther King (1929–1968)

* * *

Tony couldn't bear the evenings. He couldn't stand thinking about what was happening to Sharon. He wished that he had never seen that advert. Or if he had, that he had never shown it to her. But what could he do about it now? There had to be something. He desperately wanted to find some solution, but he felt paralysed and powerless, unable to do anything. That was why he always made sure that he was asleep when she came in. He couldn't face seeing her and knowing what he had made her do. That was why he always took the money away each morning – without saying anything to her. Then they could pretend that the events of that night hadn't really happened – and that they weren't really going to happen again the next night either.

Sharon didn't know that Tony was secretly stashing away some of the money. He wasn't sure what he was going to do with it, but he just wanted to keep it as some kind of surprise for her. And he hoped that somehow it would enable Sharon to give up the parlour. Little did he realise how soon that would happen.

They hadn't gone out looking for a business opportunity. They had never really thought of themselves as business people. But they found one that afternoon and it was to be part of the process that changed their lives.

'The Love Shack' was a shop fairly near the massage parlour. It was owned by a couple of young guys called Phil and Don. They had started it recently and were making quite a success of it. They knew what the punters wanted, and they provided it for them – films and books and magazines and various devices.

Sharon and Tony went in that day to get a new film. They used them a lot these days. In fact, they found that they could not make love with each other satisfactorily without the aid of a film or two and a line of cocaine. Without that they couldn't get the feelings they needed. It seemed as if everything felt muffled, under a cover.

Not that they really liked the word 'love' anyway –

whether it was used to describe what they did together, or in the name of the shop. Love was something else. It was something that happened in books like the one Sharon read on the plane. It was something that happened in families like the one Tony had known when he was younger. But it didn't happen here. It had nothing, absolutely nothing to do with this shop or their lives right now.

It was as Tony was paying for the film that he noticed the boxes of lacy clothes in the back room. 'What are those then, mate?' he said to Phil.

'Oh, it's just a whole load of gear I picked up cheap from a place that was closing down. But I made a big mistake there. I should have seen it first. It's too tame for our customers. You know what it's like – you want the hard stuff. You're not exactly into "naughty knickers" are you?' Tony didn't answer for a while. He was too busy thinking. 'Well, I don't know,' he said eventually. 'I might be.'

'You've got to be joking – aren't you?' said Phil with a laugh.

'I don't mean for us,' replied Tony. 'But I wonder if we might be able to sell them for you. Look, give us a couple of hours and we'll come back to you.'

Sharon looked as puzzled as Phil was. Tony ushered her out of the shop and along the pavement in the direction of their place. He didn't say anything as they walked – and whenever Sharon tried to talk to him he told her to be quiet because he was thinking.

As soon as they got to their room and walked through the door, Tony threw the film aside and started telling Sharon his plan. Back in England he had known of people, friends of his parents for instance, who sold things through 'party plans'. He explained to Sharon what this meant and told her how he reckoned that a lot of people in

Sydney would really like to use the things that shops such as 'The Love Shack' supply – but were just too embarrassed to go into them.

'So,' he said, 'this is what we do. We will set up agents who will run parties where the punters can buy stuff like "naughty knickers". And we'll make some money on that. But that's really a front, a cover, because what they will also sell is some of the harder stuff – which we can knock out at a really high price. Don't you see? People will pay because they can get it without having to face the embarrassment of going to a sex shop. And people won't be embarrassed to go to our parties because we will only advertise that they sell lingerie.'

Sharon sat and listened. She was amazed. She had no idea that Tony could think up such a brilliant plan. Within the hour they were back at the shop doing a deal with Phil. They would operate from his upstairs room for no wages but would take a percentage of all their sales. Phil called in his partner, Don, who was quite happy with the arrangement.

'Anything to shift those boxes of rubbish,' he said.

That night Tony told Sharon that he didn't want her to go to the massage parlour any more. He told her about the money he had been putting aside and how he reckoned that they could live off that until their business venture started bringing in a decent return.

As it turned out they hardly needed any of the money. The venture was a runaway success right from the beginning. They placed an advert in the paper for Party Plan Operators, and selected three of the best candidates to start with. They held their parties the next week and sold quite a lot of the lingerie – but, more important for Tony and Sharon, they sold some hard stuff too, even at their inflated prices.

Over the weeks that followed they took on more operators who held more parties. The sales snowballed. And Tony and Sharon found themselves with more money than they had ever imagined.

They bought a flash car and rented a plush apartment. Sharon chose it particularly because it had a sunken bath – something she had seen in magazines and always wanted for herself.

Of course they had to work hard. But they managed to cope by using different drugs – mainly a combination of vodka and speed so that they could keep going at the pace that was required.

13

A five-year-old was asked to define love. She said: 'It's when two people both think that they are pretty but no-one else does.'

It was a few years after I became a Christian that I first met Mike. He had come down to work at the local electricity company. That was where he met Jenny's dad, and how he ended up lodging with them for a while.

Jenny told me about him very soon after he arrived and she said that I might fancy him. I sometimes wonder how she knew that I would be interested in him. It wasn't as if we seemed suited on the surface. Almost everything about us was different. He was tall, I am short. He was quiet, I am loud. He was sport mad, I'm not the slightest bit interested in it. And so the list goes on.

But they say that opposites attract, and perhaps that's what Jenny had in mind. Anyway, we were certainly drawn to each other right from the start.

I'd never had a boyfriend before. There was one bloke who hung around Jenny's youth group – well, I suppose it became my youth group as well after that camp. Anyway this guy – Kevin, I think his name was – he came along to the group for a while. He shouldn't have really. He was a bit too old for it. But I suppose he wasn't terribly mature and he thought that he would stand a better chance of getting a girlfriend from amongst the younger girls, rather than from those of his own age. He tried it on with several of the girls, but they weren't interested. So I tried it on with him. And we spent some time together, but we never went out with each other. He obviously just didn't fancy me.

It wasn't easy to take that kind of rejection, because everyone else knew that he would go out with anyone. But not me, apparently. Can you imagine what that made me feel like? The others in the group were really nice to me about it. But I know what they were thinking, inside. And I could guess what they probably said to one another behind my back.

So, when Mike appeared and began to look in my direction I was really pleased. I couldn't believe it in fact. I didn't really know what to think. And I didn't really know what to do. I didn't want to scare him off, but I didn't want him to think that I wasn't interested either. Because I was. I really was.

Anyway, Jenny came to the rescue. She invited me round to her house and obviously tried to find some excuse or other to leave the room – so that Mike and I were left alone together. When she eventually managed to achieve that, it was actually quite embarrassing. We were all sat in Jenny's lounge where we had been listening to some music or other that she had persuaded us we really should hear. Then she said that she wanted to find another record to play for us, but that it was up in her room, and she wasn't sure how long it would take to find it – so, why didn't we just wait and chat while she went to hunt.

And that was it. Before we could answer, she was gone. It was so obvious. Mike smiled at me, but said nothing. I smiled back and started looking at the floor, wishing that it would open up and swallow me whole. But you can't stay quiet for ever – well I can't, anyway. So, eventually I looked up and started talking to him. I asked him some questions – about his work and his home and his family.

For a while it sounded a bit like an interview. I was even tempted to stop and say, 'Well, thank you very much Mr Smith, we'll be in touch with you next week to tell you if you have got the job.' I very nearly did say it. I thought it would be quite funny. But somehow I managed to stop myself.

That was the point when he began to turn the conversation round and to ask me questions about my life, and about my family. I had to make a decision when he started down that line. It was a decision that I had made many times before. And it was usually the same decision. If there was someone who I wanted to impress and they began to ask me about my home and my family, I almost always decided that I would bend the truth a bit and pretend that we were really happy and stable and secure. I had done that so many times. But recently I had felt more and more uncomfortable about doing it. And on this day I decided that I wouldn't bend the truth, or feel ashamed of my family. Whatever they were like they were my mum and dad and they had done the best they could in the circumstances, so I was going to tell it as it was. Like it or lump it I would tell Mike all about my home and my family.

And that was when I fell in love with him. It was right there, in Jenny's lounge, as I told him about my life and I saw how he reacted. He didn't say very much. He didn't need to. I could see it in his eyes. It was written all over his face. I was a battered and broken ship which had been almost sunk by the winds and waves at home and school. And he was a safe harbour who was beckoning to me, and inviting me to feel the warmth and security of his walls around me.

Over the weeks that followed, I felt those warm and secure walls around me many times, as we walked and talked, and prayed and shared our lives together.

For the first few days I couldn't believe that it was true. Each morning I woke up wondering if it was really just a dream. How many times I turned up at Jenny's home expecting to find that Mike had gone, or that he had never even existed in the first place. But he was always there, just as he had promised. Whatever he said, he did. If he arranged to meet me somewhere, then he was there, on time, ready for me. If he arranged to take me out, then he did it. He didn't forget or make an excuse at the last minute. He was there, he was always there.

As those days turned into weeks we grew closer and shared more of our lives together. As the weeks turned into months we both knew that we wanted to be as close as a man and woman ever could be – we wanted to share our whole lives together.

I don't think he ever actually asked me to marry him. Not officially. It just happened somehow, quite naturally. Over a period of time we found ourselves talking about our future lives – together. We found that we started planning what type of house we would like to have, and how many children, dogs and cats we would put inside it.

'So I suppose that means that we are going to get married, does it?' I said to him one day.

'Of course,' he replied. 'Do you think I could ever marry anyone else but you?'

'Do you really want to?' I asked.

'Look, Jacqui, if you ran away from me and tried to hide on the other side of the world, I would give up everything and travel everywhere until I had found you and married you. There's no way you are getting away from me. I want you to marry me and I want us to be together, for ever.'

It was soon after that when he bought me the engagement ring. He spent almost all the money he had on that thing. It was beautiful. I'd never held something like that, let alone had one on my finger. And now Mike had got one for me. I wanted to wear it straight away. I wanted everyone to know that we were engaged, and we were going to get married.

But Mike wouldn't let me. He said that we had to talk it through with my mum and dad first. 'Look, Jacqui, you're only seventeen. I know you want to get married to me, and I've never wanted anything as much as I want to marry you right now. But your parents might not be happy with it. They might think you are too young.'

Why was he always so sensible? And why was he always so right? 'OK,' I said, 'I agree. But let me do it. I have to choose the right time.'

And I did. I found a time when my mum and dad were together alone and I told them that Mike and I wanted to get married.

For a moment they were silent, and I waited for the whirlwind to be unleashed. But it wasn't. I could hardly believe it. I honestly thought that they would go mad at me. But they didn't. They were really pleased. I suppose they knew that Mike was just the kind of person I needed. They knew that he could give me the stability and security that I craved so much. They were hurt, obviously, that I wanted to leave home while I was so young, but they knew that I had my heart set on a new home with Mike.

With that hurdle cleared, we got engaged straight away and began planning our wedding for six months later.

It was strange wearing an engagement ring at school. The other girls really didn't know what to make of it.

'I never thought anyone would fancy her.'

'I can't believe it, is he stupid or something?'

I heard their comments, but I didn't care. For once it didn't matter to me what people said behind my back or even to my face. I was in love, and I was going to get married as soon as my A-level exams were over.

My teachers were a bit worried that I wouldn't concentrate on my school work now that I was looking forward to my wedding. But Mike was too sensible for that. He made sure that I worked hard, and he did as much as he could to prepare for our life together so that I didn't have to worry about things unnecessarily.

Mike even managed to find a small flat for us to live in when we were married. And I secured a job in an office, to start one month after our wedding.

Things couldn't have been better. It was the happiest time of my life. I had my new, secure relationship with God – and my new, secure relationship with Mike. I had a job, a home, money and friends. What more could I want? Nothing.

* * *

Phil and Don were delighted with the rapid growth of their business. Anything that made money was fine with them. Tony and Sharon liked Phil, they got on very well with him. But they weren't too sure about Don. There was something about him that set them on edge. They found out what it was one night after they had closed the shop and settled down to demolish a bottle of whisky.

They had a lot of business to discuss in preparation for the important meeting the next day. However, once they were half-way through the bottle the conversation drifted away from business and on to another topic. Don started

going on again about his spiritual beliefs. He'd talked
about them before, but never with such fervour or
commitment. It seemed that, now, he was really taking it
seriously. For years he had been playing around on the
fringes of a Satanist group in the city – and he had
gradually become increasingly involved. He told them of
his experiences of the devil, he spoke of the power he had
seen and the supernatural events that had taken place. He
suggested that they should all go along with him to see for
themselves.

As soon as they could get a word in sideways, Sharon
and Tony told Don that they weren't interested. Don
immediately turned on them and said that they didn't
know what they were rejecting. 'This is the greatest supernatural power you could imagine,' he said, with fire in his
eyes. 'I've seen the devil, I know what power he's got.'

Sharon and Tony didn't scare easily. But there was
something about Don and what he was saying that really
rattled them. The fact was that he really believed it. This
wasn't some half-hearted religious person trotting out a
sermon he'd heard in church or a story he'd learned in
Sunday School. This was a passionate believer.

For half an hour Sharon and Tony talked with Don, their
voices rising higher and higher. Phil mainly stayed out of
it, quietly finishing off the whisky. Occasionally he offered
his point of view – but the others usually ignored it and
carried on with their argument.

Eventually Sharon and Tony had had enough. They
announced that they would see the others tomorrow,
when they could get back to talking business, but right
now they were going home.

They wanted to forget about the argument they had just
had with Don. They wanted to ignore the things he had
said about the supernatural, and to get back to real life,

physical life, in this hard solid world. But they couldn't. Throughout the entire journey home they talked, without stopping, about the things that Don had said. Even when they got into their apartment and got out the vodka bottle, still they didn't stop. They turned the television on, but ignored it while they carried on talking, and then turned it off again because it was distracting them. They tried to change the subject, or just to let it drop, but they couldn't. It seemed that they were unable to think or talk about anything else.

One issue to which they seemed to keep on returning was the way in which Don had been so certain of his belief. He was so sure about the power of the devil.

'But look,' said Sharon, 'if that is all true – if there really is a devil – then there must also be a God. You can't have a devil without God, can you?'

'I guess not. You're right,' replied Tony.

'So what are we going to do about it?'

'I don't know.'

'I tell you what, if there really is a supernatural world, if there really is a God, then I want to find out about it. If there really is some kind of spiritual power then I want that,' said Sharon.

'You mean you want to go along with Don and find out about the devil?' asked Tony.

'No,' Sharon replied. 'Don't be so stupid. I want to find out about the other side. If there really is a God, then I want to find out about him.'

For some moments they sat in silence. They were both thinking the same thought, but neither had the courage to say it out loud.

'Look,' said Sharon eventually. 'Why don't you call your dad?'

'What?' said Tony.

'Call your dad,' continued Sharon. 'He'll know what to do. Tell him we want to find out about God, about Jesus, about all that kind of stuff.'

'But I can't just call him.'

'Then I will, give me the number and I'll call him right now.'

Sharon looked at Tony with determination on her face. She was a strong girl. Tough. Hard. She knew what she wanted, whatever it was.

'No,' he said. 'You can't phone him. Leave it to me. I'll do it.'

With that, Tony went straight to the phone, called the international operator and gave her the familiar number. He didn't need to look it up. It was a sequence that he had never forgotten. It was a number that he had so often wanted to call. But, in the past, he had never had the courage to go through with it. Now he did. Particularly with his wife glaring at him the way that she was.

It took some while to get through. Several attempts seemed to get nowhere. But eventually Tony heard a familiar voice at the other end.

'Hello, Dad,' he said.

'Tony – is that you?'

'Yeah, it is.'

'How lovely to hear from you. How are you, son?'

Tony briefly answered his dad's questions before he interrupted him and went straight to the point of his call.

'Look, Dad,' he said, 'we want to find out about God. We've been talking about it here for hours – and we've got to have someone who can help us. Do you know anyone over here? We want to meet with a Christian. We've got a lot we want to find out.'

'Sure, son,' said Tony's dad.

'Of course I'm sure, that's why I'm phoning you.'

'No, sorry,' said his dad, 'the line's bad, we're not hearing each other properly. I didn't ask whether you were sure – I just said . . .'

Tony's dad didn't really know what to say. The fact was that it was just too much to take in so quickly. It was hard to think. It was hard to speak. But he had to keep going, he must try to keep his voice sounding steady and he must ignore the tears that were beginning to run down his cheeks.

'Of course I'll put you in touch with someone. Look – just give me your phone number and I'll get it organised straight away. Someone will phone you as soon as they can.'

'Thanks, Dad.'

They didn't quite know what else to say once Tony had given his dad the number. They talked for a bit. But really they both wanted to get off the phone so that his dad could find someone to contact them.

Of course it wasn't as easy as his dad had expected. When he worked out what time it was in Australia he realised that his son had been calling in the middle of the night and there wouldn't be many people awake for him to call.

However, he called his local Christian bookshop. He knew that they had branches all over the world, with people who were always happy to talk. The bookshop gave him the number of their head office and when he phoned them they gave him the number of a bookshop in Sydney. But they told him, in no uncertain terms, exactly what time it was over there and suggested that, unless it was an absolute emergency, he should leave it a good few hours. So he did. He calculated the time difference and worked out the time that he would call. He now had several hours to wait.

But he didn't sit around. He called the family into the

room. And, huddled together in the lounge, they began to pray.

'Please, Lord, show them that you love them . . .'

'Please, Lord, let them know that your arms are always open wide for them . . .'

'Please, Lord, bring them back to you . . .'

'Please, Lord . . . Please, Lord . . . Please, Lord . . .'

And so the prayers went on, minute after minute, hour after hour, without stopping.

Even when it was time for Tony's dad to call the manager of the bookshop in Sydney; even as he spoke to him on the phone; even when the manager was calling Tony and Sharon; they kept on praying.

Meanwhile, in Australia, the couple they were praying for had crashed out on the bed. Since calling Tony's dad they had sat by the phone, waiting for it to ring. They hadn't talked much more. They had simply sat and looked at the phone. However, as they waited, they became aware of their tiredness. Their eyelids became heavy. First Sharon went to lie down on the bed. Then Tony joined her. Soon they were both fast asleep – worn out from their long conversation, and practically unconscious from the amount of whisky and vodka they had consumed.

When, eventually, the telephone did ring the two sleeping bodies hardly stirred. It rang for a long time. But neither of them woke up. A few minutes later it rang again. This time they turned over and began to rouse out of their stupor. But somehow, as much as they wanted to answer it, they couldn't drag their bodies awake enough. In their minds they wanted to get up, but their bodies just wouldn't move. They felt stuck, unable to respond, until the ringing stopped once more and they fell back into a deep sleep.

It was some hours later when they did eventually stir.

They were still dressed in their clothes from the night before – which were now crumpled and wet with sweat. Their mouths were dry and their heads throbbed. But most of all, they felt embarrassed. As they lay still they each remembered the events of the night before. Had it really happened? Had they really talked like that? Had they actually phoned Tony's dad? Had they really said that they wanted to find out about God and Jesus and all that stuff?

They didn't know what to say to each other. So they said nothing. They each peeled off their damp, sticky clothes, fell into a bath and got dressed in silence. Sharon drained the last few drops from the bottle of vodka that was still by the phone, while Tony snorted something up his nose. Then they both grabbed some chocolate and ran to the car, clutching the map that told them how to get to the solicitor's office.

'The Love Shack' business had grown so much recently that Phil and Don had decided that they should turn it into a limited company. That required a lot of negotiation because a major reason for the growth of the company was the success of Tony and Sharon's part of the business. They had a deal with one another about how they were sharing out the profits but that now had to be renegotiated if the business was to be incorporated.

Tony and Sharon were late for the meeting and by the time they arrived Phil and Don had already decided, together with the solicitor, what they should offer them.

'We've looked at it very carefully,' said the grey-haired man with the black suit, 'and we want to offer you a 10 per cent shareholding in the company. We think that this is very fair and reasonable in view of the current situation.'

'Well we don't think it is at all,' said Sharon, without even looking at Tony. 'It's us that have made this company.

We think that we should have at least 30 per cent of the shares.'

The solicitor coughed to himself. 'I really don't think that is possible,' he said, looking at Phil and Don, who both shook their heads in a way that they hoped would not be noticed by Tony and Sharon.

For the next hour they tried to negotiate together. It wasn't easy for any of them. Tony and Sharon did not want to move from the figure of 30 per cent – and neither did Phil and Don want to move from their figure of 10 per cent.

Eventually the solicitor said, 'Well, I think all that I can suggest is that we meet together again on Friday at the same time. That will give us all two days to think it over.'

They agreed on this and left the office. Phil and Don went to open up the shop, while Tony and Sharon drove back to their apartment. On the way they discussed how they would persuade the others to increase their offer; and how, if they didn't win that battle, they would start up on their own. They knew that they held all the cards, no matter how much Phil and Don tried to bluff them. Sure, they could make more money by carrying on as part of the established company, but if they had to they could start their own company. They knew everything about their party plan business. And it was them that their customers knew, so if they had to go it alone they would come with them. Either way, they were in control. They were in charge. They had a battle to fight, but they knew that they were going to win.

They continued to discuss the strength of their position as they climbed the stairs. And they were still deep in conversation as they opened the door. So they didn't, at first, notice the phone ringing. In fact, by the time Tony eventually picked up the receiver the line had gone dead.

'Who was it?' called out Sharon.

'I don't know – perhaps it was Phil or Don, or the solicitor, with another offer. Look, we need to be clear on our tactics here. Let's sit down and work out a battle plan.'

'OK. But first of all I need another drink. Did we really finish all that vodka last night? Look, I'll nip out and get another bottle while you work out some kind of strategy.'

With that, Sharon was gone. Tony heard her footsteps down the stairs, until they were drowned out by the sound of the phone ringing again. This time he got to it immediately – and heard a voice that he didn't recognise.

'Is that Tony?' the voice said.

'Yeah.'

'Great, I was beginning to think that I'd been given the wrong number. You don't know me, but my name's Clive. I run the local Christian bookshop and I got a phone call this morning from your dad, in England.'

'Oh . . . er . . . yes,' said Tony hesitantly.

'He said that you would like someone to talk to – about God and things.'

'Yes, er no, er we did. But that was last night. It's different now.'

'Really? Are you sure? You know your dad went to an awful lot of trouble to find me and to ask me if I would contact you.'

'I suppose he did.'

'So don't you think that you owe it to him to follow it through?'

'No. Well, yeah, I guess I do.'

'How about tonight then, can we meet up?'

'No, we're busy. That's no good, sorry.'

'Well what about tomorrow night – you can't be busy then as well?'

'Well actually we . . . no, we're not. We can make it

tomorrow night. Look, give me your address and we'll be there – say 8 p.m.?'

'Fine, I'll look forward to it.'

Tony wrote down the address and stuffed it in his pocket. He didn't plan to take it out again. He thought he would just let the day pass and then throw the piece of paper away. When Sharon returned he didn't say anything to her about the call. He reckoned that she had probably gone as cold on the idea as he had, and he thought it was best just to let it drop.

The problem was that Clive didn't let it drop. He phoned back at about 7 p.m. the next day, to confirm that the meeting was on. Only this time Sharon answered. When she found out that Tony had arranged for them to go to see some crazy Christian without telling her, she was livid.

14

There are two ways to get enough: one is to continue to accumulate more. The other is to desire less.

G. K. Chesterton (1874–1936)

'What do you think you're doing?' said Sharon to her husband.

Tony didn't quite know what to say. Which way should he jump? In the end he said, 'Well, the other night we did want to find out about God. We did ask Dad to find someone for us to talk to.'

'I know, but that was then, this is now. Things change.'

'Yes, but he obviously went to a lot of trouble setting this up. I think the least we can do is to go through with it. Besides, if we don't, I think this guy Clive is going to be calling us every day.'

'OK then,' said Sharon, 'we'll go and get it over with. Just let me get ready.'

So she did get ready – in the same way that she did when she had gone to visit Tony's dad. Only this time her clothes were more expensive and more provocative.

'What do you reckon he'll look like?' asked Sharon as they drove across to the other side of town.

'How should I know?'

'I reckon he'll be wearing a cardigan and will have a side-parting and glasses,' said Sharon, adding yet another layer to her lipstick. Tony laughed and nodded his head.

They found Clive's house quite easily. They even found that they recognised him when he opened the door. Because there he was – with a side-parting and glasses, and wearing a cardigan.

'Do come in,' he said. 'It's so nice to meet you.'

Sharon looked around as she entered the house. She had heard of make-do-and-mend but this was ridiculous. Didn't these people have any money? What proper furniture they had was obviously fourth, fifth or sixth hand. And some of their 'tables' weren't even tables at all – just boxes with a cloth over the top.

'This is Cindy,' Clive said, introducing his wife.

'It's so nice to meet you, let me get you a drink,' she added.

Cindy and Sharon couldn't have been further apart in their appearance. But Cindy never criticised her, not even with her eyes or her facial expression. She just seemed to accept her exactly as she was. Sharon sensed again exactly the same feeling that she had known when she had visited Tony's parents. Here were people that knew what love really was. Here were people who could welcome and accept someone into their home – and treat them with a dignity and a respect that they had never known. Here were people who had nothing and yet had everything.

They talked for a while in a way that people do when they first meet someone else at a party. Cindy asked how long they had been in Australia and what they thought of Sydney. Tony asked them where their shop was and how business was doing.

Clive explained that they weren't really worried about how much business they did – just how many people they were able to help. 'A lot of our customers don't buy any books at all – they just come in because they need someone to talk to,' he explained.

'So how do you make your money?' asked Tony.

'We don't really. We're not in it to make money,' said Cindy.

That explains a lot, thought Sharon to herself.

'Anyway, that's enough about us,' said Clive. 'Let's talk about you. I'm fascinated to know what led you to call your dad and ask him to put you in touch with some Christians.'

'Oh, it wasn't anything much really. We just thought we wanted to find out something about God, that was all.' Sharon felt embarrassed as she said it, and looked at the door, wondering whether it might be simpler in the long run just to get up and leave now.

'So,' said Clive, leaning forward in his chair and looking at Sharon with an obvious warmth and friendship that made her feel at once comfortable and uncomfortable, 'what do you think of Jesus?'

'What do I think of Jesus? What a question! I think he's a figment of everyone's imagination,' Sharon replied.

'You know,' said Clive, 'a lot of people have that idea. But I don't really know where they get it from, because there is actually no real doubt that Jesus existed.'

Sharon said nothing, but raised an eyebrow in a way that said, 'Go on then – convince me.'

Over the next few hours Clive and Cindy did convince her, and Tony as well. They explained about the historical evidence for the existence of Christ, and his miracles, and his resurrection from the dead. They told their guests how they believed that the life and teaching of Jesus is not just some fairy-tale – but that it is actually true. And they invited them to explore it for themselves.

So Tony and Sharon fired questions at these Christians relentlessly.

'Hasn't the Bible changed over the years?' asked Sharon.

'How can miracles be possible?' asked Tony.

'But hasn't science disproved Christianity!' objected Sharon.

Initially their questions were hostile and aggressive. There were times when Clive was a bit worried that they were going to stand up and storm out. But no matter how truculent Sharon and Tony became, he and Cindy always responded with a quiet graciousness that simply flowed naturally out their hearts – because of their growing love for their guests.

It was actually that behaviour which impressed the questioners most of all – not the answers they gave, so much as the way that they gave them.

Nothing seems to rattle them thought Tony to himself. *They seem to be completely confident that their faith will hold together no matter what anyone throws at it.*

They're not just talking about love and forgiveness Sharon thought to herself *they're actually living it out – showing it to us right now. Who do we think we are – being so rude and aggressive to them in their own home? And yet they're just sitting there and taking it. And loving us. And accepting us.*

After about an hour of this barrage of antagonistic questions and objections, the atmosphere changed. No-one said anything to cause it. It just seemed to happen on its own. Somehow Sharon and Tony stopped attacking their hosts and seemed, instead, to stand alongside them. They asked questions that were just as searching and demanding. But now they were clearly intending to find out about the message of Jesus and not to demolish it – indeed they had discovered that there was no point trying to knock it down, because it seemed that it could stand up to anything they would throw.

It was very late in the evening when Sharon eventually asked a question that had been on her mind for quite a while.

'Look,' she said. 'If I did become a Christian, tell me – what would I have to give up?'

Cindy smiled at her and replied, 'We can't tell you that, Sharon.'

'Why ever not?' asked Tony. 'You've answered every other question we've asked – why not this one?'

'Because,' said Clive, 'it's not for us, or any other Christian, to tell you that. It's not our job to run your life or to tell you what to do. God will show you, at the right time.'

'Oh come on – how is God going to show us?' asked Sharon.

'Well, you remember what I said earlier about becoming a Christian meaning that you come into a relationship with God – so you don't just know about him, you also know him?' said Clive.

'Yes,' said Sharon. It had taken quite a while, earlier in the evening, for her to grasp what that meant. Somehow she had always assumed that Christians were people who followed a list of rules; she didn't realise that being a Christian was really all about knowing God. Tony, however, already understood what that meant, because he had experienced something of the presence of God that afternoon with his dad, all those years ago.

'Well, when you live in that relationship with God he will show you what things you need to change.'

'But how?' insisted Sharon.

'Sometimes it will be through the Bible. It's like a letter from God to us and sometimes you will find that God will speak to you very clearly through it. Other times it might be through the conscience that God will re-awaken within you. There are many different ways that God can speak to people who want to hear him. You'll know. You won't need us to tell you. If you really love God with all your heart then he will show you the right path – and you will find that you want to follow it.'

Ama Deum et fac quod vis (Love God and do what you want).

Augustine of Hippo (345–430)

It is God who works in you to will and to act according to his good purpose.

St Paul (Philippians 2:13)

'But why do we need to change? Why can't we just carry on as we are?' There wasn't much conviction in Sharon's voice as she asked that question. She knew that she didn't want to stay the way that she was. Just being with Clive and Cindy that evening and hearing about Jesus, made her acutely aware of how desperately she wanted to change. Sure, she had all the money she could want, and all the drugs – and all the sex too, for that matter. But she knew that there must be more to life than this. In her heart, or what was left of it, she longed to be soft again, she longed to feel again, she longed to be clear and clean and pure.

'God loves us and he wants the very best for us. He doesn't want to see us hurting ourselves or others. So that is why he wants us to change – so that we can stop doing the things that damage us and other people.'

Sharon didn't even open her mouth to object to Clive's answer. How could she? She knew that it was true, she just wished that she wasn't quite so scared of change. In actual fact it wasn't change that she was worried about so much as an inability to change. She wanted to be different, she wanted to be set free from her attitudes and habits and weaknesses. She just couldn't see how it could happen. She was scared that she would be let down again – and find that the change that Clive was talking about just wasn't possible for her.

'Look,' continued Clive, 'at this precise moment God isn't asking you to give up anything. He is not giving you a list of things and saying, "Give those up and then come back and see me." What he is doing is to say, "Are you prepared to change? Are you willing to follow me, whatever the cost?" At the minute you don't know what that will be. I didn't, the day I became a Christian. I just knew that I wanted to follow Jesus; I wanted to be with him and to do whatever he asked me to do. Then you will find that he will gradually change you. You don't have to do anything except be willing for God to work supernaturally in your life, changing you from the inside out.'

Tony looked at Sharon. Nervously, and slowly, he nodded at her. It was just a small nod. If you didn't know him you might not even have noticed it. But Sharon did. And she nodded back.

'Look,' she said, to everyone in the room, 'I don't want any Sunday morning faith. I don't want to be a hypocrite who behaves in one way on one day and quite differently through the rest of the week. If I am going to go for this then I'm going to go for it all the way. One hundred per cent. No holding back. You know what I mean?'

'That's my girl,' said Tony with a smile. 'She's right, you know. If we do this we do it together and we do it for keeps.'

'So let's do it,' said Sharon.

And they did. Both of them knelt down side by side in Clive and Cindy's room, and they prayed. Neither of them prayed very complicated prayers. Cindy had told them not to worry about that anyway. God didn't really care about the words they used, it was the attitude of their hearts and minds that mattered most.

'After all,' said Cindy, 'the thief who was dying on the cross next to Jesus simply prayed, "Jesus, remember me when you come into your kingdom," and Jesus told him, "Today you will be with me in paradise." His prayer wasn't very flowery but he meant it, and God heard it.'

In their different ways Sharon and Tony told God that they were sorry for all the wrong that they had done, and asked him to forgive them. They told him that from then on they wanted to follow Jesus and to serve him, whatever the cost. And they asked him to come and live inside them, to cleanse them, and to enable them to live for him.

When they had finished praying, Cindy and Clive drew alongside them, placed their hands lightly on their shoulders and prayed for them.

At the time Sharon didn't know what was happening. All she knew was that something was lifting off her. She could feel it. Almost physically she could sense a weight being taken away. And inside, she felt something begin to break. Somehow, she didn't know how, God had started to melt her hardened heart. For the first time in years Sharon felt her eyes begin to fill with tears. She didn't try to stop them. She didn't even wipe them away as they flowed down her cheeks. She just let them go.

Until that point Tony hadn't felt very much at all. He knew that something had changed within him. He knew that from now on he was determined to follow Jesus wherever that took him. And he knew that he must start by putting the drugs right out of his life as soon as possible. He knew what he had to do, and he was going to do it. But he couldn't really say that he had any emotional feeling at all.

However, the sound and sight of Sharon crying beside him changed all that. His own tears seemed to well up from deep within him as he lent over and put his arms around her. Immediately Sharon turned towards him and melted into his chest in a way that he had never previously known in all the time that they had been together. Of course they had held each other before, many times. But that was different. Never, in all that time, had she ever let herself go into his arms like this, never had she seemed so soft or so warm.

Clive and Cindy sat back and waited patiently until the time was right for them to speak to their guests again.

Eventually, when Tony and Sharon released each other and turned round, Clive smiled at them and said gently, 'Becoming a Christian affects different people in so many different ways. For you it has obviously been quite an emotional experience. That's not surprising, because it has all been so quick. But I need to make sure that you understand that following Jesus is not based upon feelings. You will find that your feelings will come and go. What is important is that you know that you have made a commitment to God that you want to follow Jesus with all of your life. He will lead you, he will guide you. Sometimes you will be very aware of his presence with you. You may find that there are times when God feels so close that you could almost reach out and touch him. At other times he will seem as if he is a million miles away. But he is still there, he won't leave you.'

That was the first of many pieces of advice that Clive and Cindy gave them that night. It seemed that they had more questions now than they had before they became Christians. They tried to ask as many as they could. But Clive soon pointed out how late it was, and suggested that they should go home to bed.

'There was one question we didn't ask them,' said Sharon as they started the car and waved back at Clive and Cindy.

'Just one? There are loads,' said Tony.

'Yeah, but one in particular. What do we do about the meeting with the solicitor tomorrow morning?'

He is no fool who gives up what he cannot keep, to gain what he cannot lose.

Jim Elliot (1927–1956)

For where your treasure is, there your heart will be also.

Jesus Christ (Matthew 6:21)

'We've changed our minds,' said Sharon.

'You've what?'

'We've changed our minds,' continued Tony. 'I know what we said before and how definite we were about it. But the fact is that we don't want to go on with it.'

'So what do you want now? Fifty per cent? Sixty?' said Phil, with an undisguised note of sarcasm in his voice.

'No – nothing.'

'What do you mean, nothing?'

'He means just what he said – nothing. We don't want any shares. We're leaving the business. We don't want anything more to do with it. Here are our keys. And here are the books that we kept at home. That's everything. It's all yours now. We're out of it.'

Sharon stood up as she handed over the books and keys, and Tony followed behind her as she headed for the door.

But Don got there ahead of them both.

'Now hang on a minute. What's your game? What are you up to?' he said.

'Nothing. We just want out, that's all,' replied Tony.

'No, you're up to something. What is it? You're going to set up somewhere else, aren't you?' Don continued. 'You're going to run something on your own to compete with us.'

'We're not. We've just had enough of the business. We're leaving it. And we're leaving here now.'

'You're not going anywhere until we know what is going on,' said Don.

'Actually,' the grey-haired solicitor interrupted, 'we can't hold them against their will if they want to go.'

'Shut up,' said Phil, as he lifted his right hand. For a moment it looked as if he was going to strike the solicitor with the back of his hand. But he clearly thought again and, instead, just wiped it across his mouth slowly and deliberately, as he thought deeply. 'Look,' he said, 'Tony and Sharon don't mind hanging on here for a little while until we straighten this out, do you?'

They said nothing.

'Now, all we want to know is – what are you going to do?'

'We told you,' said Tony. 'We're leaving the business.'

'What, just like that? Overnight? Suddenly everything changes. What's got into you guys?'

'Nothing,' said Sharon.

'I don't like it,' said Don. 'I don't like it at all.'

'Well that's your problem isn't it, mate?' replied Tony.

'I. wonder if I might make a suggestion here,' interrupted the solicitor very cautiously. 'If you say that you are not going to set up your own business, will you sign a "non-competition" contract?'

'Sure we will,' said Tony.

And so they did. Phil and Don just didn't know what to make of it. The solicitor found it hard to believe that they would sign away their rights to all that money. But he was a lawyer and not a psychiatrist, so he simply drew up a very short document, and they signed it there and then.

'Now,' said Tony, as he laid down the pen and followed Sharon through the door, 'you can just leave us alone.'

As soon as the door closed behind them, Sharon turned to him and said, 'That's it then. There's no going back now.'

'Well, that was what we decided,' replied Tony. 'We made up our minds last night, and we're going to stick to it.'

Indeed it was what they had decided. Even before they had driven half-way home from Clive and Cindy's house, they had agreed together what they were going to do. It didn't take much discussion. They had both, actually, made the decision on their own before they had even got into the car. They knew that they couldn't carry on in that business. They both knew that they had to get out.

They also both knew that they had to clear out all of their drugs. They had spent too much of their time dependent upon these chemicals and now they had the opportunity to be free. So that night they stood over their toilet bowl and poured in a range of tablets and powders. They didn't find it difficult. They had often privately dreamed of this moment – when they could turn their backs for ever on the drugs that had been so much a part of their lives during the last few years.

They didn't have any second thoughts as they saw the drugs in the bottom of the water, waiting to be flushed away. They didn't want to hold any back in case they changed their minds. They knew that this was going to be the end of drugs in their lives for ever. At least they were sure of this until they came to the cannabis. They had both left it to last. Now, when all of their tablets and powders were waiting to be sent to the sewers, somehow Tony couldn't put the cannabis in as well. He hesitated as he held it in his hand. He looked at Sharon. He could see that she wasn't sure either.

'Look, I don't know about this,' said Tony.

'No, nor do I,' added Sharon. 'I think we should hold on to this stuff.'

'I agree. It has never been a problem. We can handle it OK.'

'Yeah. We can always ask Clive what he thinks we should do about it.'

They never did ask Clive. Although for the next few months they seemed to be round his house practically every day, they didn't tell him that they were still using cannabis. They carried on smoking it for months – until, strangely enough, one night they were sitting in a pub smoking a joint and talking to a student about how they had become Christians. The student leant across to them and said, 'How can you talk to me about Jesus with a joint in your hand?' And he was right. How could they? That night they gave up the last of their drugs.

That was when they also decided that the time had come for them to go home. They had often thought about it. Ever since they had driven home from Clive and Cindy's on the night that had changed their lives. The first thing they had done when they had opened the door was to phone Tony's dad and mum, and tell them what had happened. Since then they had called as often as they could. And now they knew that they must go back to England. Each of them must be properly reconciled to their families. They knew that they had to do it. Tony looked forward to seeing his mum and dad. Many times he imagined falling at his dad's feet and saying how sorry he had been. He imagined hugging his mum and holding on to her.

And Sharon wished that her family would be as pleased with their news as Tony's was. But she knew that it was unlikely that her wish would come true.

'Do you remember when we arrived here?' Tony said, as they sat together in the airport lounge.

'Yeah, it's as clear to me in my mind as if it were yesterday,' replied Sharon. 'I can even remember exactly what I was thinking. I couldn't think of anything else. Here we were in a new land to start our new life. It was going to be different. We were going to be free. It was what I had always wanted.'

'It didn't last long, did it?'

'No, it . . .'

'Will passengers for British Airways flight 308 to London, England, please go to gate 12.'

The announcement broke into their conversation. They stood up and looked at Clive and Cindy. They didn't know what to say. And if they had known, they wouldn't have been able to say it. They simply hugged each other one last time. Cindy tried not to cry. And failed. Clive tried to think of something profound with which to send them off. But couldn't. In the end they just smiled at each other and waved as Tony and Sharon walked through the door on the start of their journey home.

* * *

It was a long journey. And it didn't seem to stop when they arrived back in England. They continued to grow and change and develop in their faith day by day, and week by week.

Initially they lived at the vicarage with Tony's mum and dad. They spent a lot of time studying the Bible – and helping others to do so. They prayed as much as they could – and they helped others to pray.

No matter where they were or what they were doing, they were always seeking to lead others to faith in Christ. And when they were with other Christians they were always seeking to help them to grow in their faith.

Tony's dad watched their lives develop. He saw how they gave themselves so much to other people. And he knew that God was calling them into the ministry. Tony and Sharon were aware of it too.

So it wasn't long before Tony was applying to theological colleges.

When he was finally accepted on to a course, he found that it wasn't quite what he had expected. He and Sharon didn't have an easy time of it. They enjoyed being with other Christians who wanted to learn more about the Bible and how they could help others to be set free through a radical encounter with God. But they weren't exactly the typical 'Rev and Mrs' in the making. They were still very rough. They still liked their cigarettes. They still carried the scars from their lives.

But they were one hundred per cent committed to serving God and to serving others. So they found that people loved them and accepted them. Especially when they graduated and were sent out to their first church.

Tony became the curate of a lively church in the south of England. They settled in quickly and became close friends with a number of the other young couples. In fact, this was one of their special responsibilities in the church – to help young couples to grow in their love for each other and for God.

15

I am convinced that neither death nor life, neither angels nor demons, neither the present nor the future, nor any powers, neither height nor depth, nor anything else in all creation, will be able to separate us from the love of God that is in Christ Jesus our Lord.

St Paul (Romans 8:38–39)

We spent our honeymoon in Dorset, walking around the cliff paths and over the hills. Mike had always loved outdoor exercise. I must say that I wasn't so keen. But then I wasn't anywhere near as fit as him. On most days Mike had to encourage me along and even pull me up the hills. Sometimes I sat on a bench at the bottom while he climbed up some footpath or rocky slope so that he could get a better view over the fields or across the sea.

But even though I couldn't always keep up with his pace, I loved being there with him. And I loved the thought of returning, at the end of our honeymoon, to our new flat and our new life together.

When we did get back we spent many evenings entertaining our friends to meals on our new table, laid out with our new crockery. I'd never known anything like this – having matching sets of plates and bowls, in a wonderfully stable home.

Suddenly I felt so grown up, not a schoolgirl any more, but a married woman with a home to run. Mike and I began taking responsibility for leading some of the youth activities in the church. We really enjoyed working together in that way – and knowing that we were doing something that could make a difference to other people's lives.

I also started meeting up with some of the other married women at the church. I became particularly friendly with a girl called Julia who had also recently got married. Her husband used to have some high-pressure job in the city, but had given it all up and was now working in a home for maladjusted kids. She was a teacher and her school was near my office so we sometimes met for lunch in the local sandwich bar.

It was during one of those lunches that we talked about the walks Mike and I had enjoyed on our honeymoon. And Julia said that she and her husband had often talked about going away for a weekend hiking in the countryside – so why didn't we go together? I said I thought that it was a great idea and I was sure that Mike would be keen on it to.

When I told Mike about it I could see that he wasn't so sure. I was really puzzled by that. I didn't quite know what to make of it. For some reason he didn't seem to want to talk to me about it.

'Is it the fact that I've suggested going with another couple?'

'No, it's not that.'

'Is it the money?'

'No, it's none of that,' he said. 'Look, it's nothing. It's just that I don't feel terribly keen on walking at the moment.'

'But you love walking, you always have.'

'I know, it's just that – well, you know I haven't felt very well recently, that's all. But if you want to go, then we'll go.'

'No, if you'd rather not, then I'll tell Julia that it's off.'

'Look, we're not starting all this nonsense of arguing the other way round now. Let's go. Perhaps it will do me good. It may be just what I need to clear this chest.'

Well, he certainly did need something to pick him up at the moment. He'd had some kind of flu, or perhaps it was bronchitis. We didn't really know. It had started soon after we came back from honeymoon. I tried to get him to go to the doctor, but you know what men are like. He didn't want to make a fuss. The trouble was that he didn't seem to be getting any better. He said that he just needed some time to get his strength back. Well, he didn't take any time off work, he just took it easy at home in the evenings. Actually that suited me. I loved just staying in with him, and having friends round. But now I really did want to get out and go away for this weekend. So I was glad that he had agreed. And I knew it would do him good.

On the Friday evening, some weeks later, we packed the car and drove down to a beautiful little village by the sea. Julia and Andy travelled down separately and we met up as arranged in the hotel's little restaurant. We sat at a table in the corner, beneath the oak beams and by the leaded windows. It was a lovely meal, and I remember thinking how lucky I was to have such good friends and such a wonderful husband. Afterwards we all sat round the roaring log fire in the hotel lounge, drinking fruit wines and chatting about everything and nothing. It was one of the most relaxing, enjoyable evenings that I had ever known.

As the fire burned down and the evening drew to a

close, Andy got out the map and suggested that we plan our route for the next day. He was keen on climbing up some of the hills, but Mike persuaded him that it might be a good idea to take it more easily on the first day. That was obviously a bit of a disappointment to Andy but he accepted it graciously and so, the next day, after breakfast, we all set off on quite a gentle walk along the coastal path.

There were some slopes, of course, but nothing too steep, nothing that even I would struggle with. That was when I knew that something was wrong. Because Mike found it very difficult to keep up. Andy and Julia went on ahead while Mike and I fell further and further behind.

'I'm OK,' he told me every time I asked him, 'just a bit wheezy, that's all. I need to take it slowly but I'll be fine. Don't worry.'

However, I could see that he wasn't fine. And I did worry. We completed the walk, but we had to take it slowly, very slowly.

When we eventually got back to the hotel, Julia and Andy were already eating lunch in the lounge. 'We didn't know whether to wait for you two love-birds.' They said. 'We thought that you might be wanting more time on your own.'

'No,' I said, 'we didn't hang back to be on our own. It was just that . . . '

'It was nothing, I just . . .'

'Look, Mike,' I interrupted, 'I've had enough of you saying that it's nothing. There is something wrong. You could hardly walk out there. You had to keep stopping to get your breath back. You can't go on like this.'

'But it's just the effects of that flu, or whatever it was. Or perhaps it's asthma. I don't know. It will pass. I'll get better.'

But he didn't get better. Wherever we walked that weekend, Mike struggled to keep up. We all became very concerned about him. And eventually he agreed that he would go to the doctor as soon as we got home.

The doctor asked a few questions and listened to his chest for a while before writing out a prescription and telling Mike that this should fix it. It seemed that Mike had often had chest infections when he was a boy, and there was one time when he had a series of recurrent attacks of bronchitis, so the doctor thought that this was just an old problem returning.

Mike dutifully took the tablets that he had been prescribed, but they made him no better. In fact, if anything, he was worse. He must have had three or four different sets of tablets before the doctor decided to refer him to a specialist at the hospital. By then his condition had deteriorated even further.

I guess that when something develops gradually, bit by tiny bit, you don't notice the changes – you just get used to them, and accept them. Well, I certainly noticed them on the day of his hospital appointment. I remember that we couldn't park in the hospital grounds so we had to leave the car down one of the back-streets. It was then quite a steep walk up the hill to get to the hospital reception. Mike could hardly manage it. He kept stopping. He even had to sit down on the pavement for a while at one point. I wanted to go back and get the car so that I could drive him right up to the door. But he wouldn't have any of that. He kept saying that he was OK, and that he was going to make it alright. Pig-headed and stubborn he was – all the time.

When we eventually got to the receptionist, we were late and had missed the appointment. But they seemed to be very understanding and they said that they could just reschedule him for later that afternoon.

We spent the next hour or so idly thumbing through the magazines. All this hanging around made us feel frustrated and I, particularly, became quite cross. All we wanted was the right medicine to get Mike back to health again – so that we could get on with our lives. We had plans, we had places to go and things to do. And we wanted to get on with them right now.

We anticipated that we would walk out of that hospital that afternoon with a piece of paper in our hands – and that this would be our ticket back to a normal life. That was what we had come for. That was what we expected. But it wasn't what we got.

As soon as the specialist saw Mike she admitted him straight to a ward. I remember walking with him as he was taken through the hospital in a wheelchair. We passed other patients who were being moved around on chairs or beds – many of them carried drips or were even only semi-conscious. I tried to hold Mike's hand. But it wasn't easy. I couldn't always keep up with the chair. I tried not to worry, I tried not to cry. But that was even harder.

I suppose that it was partly the suddenness of it all, the shock. We had planned a meal for that night. Jenny and her new boyfriend were coming over. We were going to use that new fondue set. I had bought a new dress and I wanted to show it to her.

But we never did have that meal. We never did use that fondue set. Our life was never to be the same again.

In the days that followed they ran every kind of test that they could. Everything that could be analysed was analysed. Then the consultant arranged to see me and Mike together.

'I'm afraid it's not good news,' she said, holding up some pictures. 'Can you see here? Your lungs are covered in clots. Look, here and here. There are multiple blood clots on both sides of your lungs.'

I didn't know what it meant, but I could tell that it wasn't good. Neither of us said anything for a while. We just stared at the little marks on the pictures.

I don't know what Mike was thinking. I didn't get a chance to ask him. The consultant continued with her explanation.

'The trouble is, Mike, that your lungs can't actually work properly. That is then putting a lot of pressure on your heart.' She frowned. 'To be honest with you, this is not a common condition. And I'm not really sure what to do with it.'

At that point she obviously saw the expression on my face. I hadn't expected her to say that she didn't know what to do. She was a doctor, for goodness sake, a consultant, a specialist. She had to know what to do. It was her job. Couldn't we just get rid of the clots? Couldn't she put some kind of cloth inside him to polish him up? It's strange, the odd thoughts that go through your mind at a time like that.

'Now, don't worry,' she continued, 'although I'm not really familiar with this condition, others are. We need to bring in some other people who have dealt with this before. We'll do some phoning around and let you know.'

At this point Mike started asking questions. He'd obviously been formulating them in his mind. She did her best to answer them, but she was clearly out of her depth. She kept saying, 'I don't know.'

But we needed to know. So we kept asking. We asked the nurses, we asked the doctors, we even asked the cleaners if they knew what was happening. None of them could tell us anything much, except that Mike was very sick and that they were looking at ways in which the condition could be contained. None of them ever mentioned the word 'cure'. None of them ever talked about him getting well again, or leaving the hospital. They just kept talking about 'containing the condition' and 'managing his symptoms'.

They put Mike in a different ward. This one had three other men, who all looked much weaker than him. I felt quite annoyed by that. What was Mike doing there? I asked myself. He should be home with me, not here amongst the sick and the dying. We should be planning our home and our family – not waiting in a ward. We'd only been married for such a short time. We wanted to be together. We had plans. We had hopes and dreams for the future. And we wanted to be getting on with them now.

But we had to wait. For week after week, as they continued to run tests, and as different teams of doctors examined him. Each time they pulled back the bedclothes to look, I noticed how much thinner he had become. Every time they asked him to breath into some machine or other, I noticed how much weaker his lungs were. His eyes seemed to have sunk back into his head, his skin had became pale and his hair hung limply over his head.

Mike's parents came down and he broke into tears when he saw them. I'd never seen him look so young or vulnerable. Here was the man who was my rock, my safe harbour, my solid shelter, and he was crying in his mother's arms like a little boy who was helpless and hopeless. They prayed for him, and with him. And so did I.

In fact a lot of people came and prayed with us. Particularly Tony. He was our new curate. He and his wife Sharon had recently arrived in the parish. It was their first post since they had left theological college. They weren't exactly your average 'Rev and Mrs'. They had obviously been through a lot before they had become Christians, and somehow they seemed to bear the scars. Perhaps that was why they had become such warm and loving people. They understood. They cared.

They certainly loved us and cared for us. They came in every day, to pray with us. They were also really good friends with Andy and Julia. And so the six of us spent a lot of time together around and on Mike's bed. We talked together, we prayed together. We told stories about our lives to one another.

Sharon and Julia, in particular, tried to keep me cheerful. Julia brought in food and Sharon kept us supplied with magazines and books. They even took me out shopping one day, while Andy and Tony stayed with Mike. It seemed so strange to be out in the real world again. The high street was full of shoppers bustling around in their busy lives, unaware that just a few miles away, in the hospital, a man was lying in bed, so ill.

I bought a new dress that afternoon and Sharon dropped me off with it at the hospital. I thought that it would help Mike to see what I had found – to help him to look forward to the times we could have together when he got well again. I held it up against me as I walked through the door into his ward.

'Tadaa!' I said. 'What do you think of this, then? It'll be your "welcome home" dress. I'll wear it to the party we'll have when you get better.'

Mike tried hard to look at it and to seem interested. But it was too much for him. He just couldn't summon up enough enthusiasm for it. He tried to be pleased for me, but he just couldn't do it.

I knelt down beside his bed, laying my head on his lap. Mike lifted his hand and placed it lightly on my hair, which he then stroked gently.

The doctor stood silently behind me. He knew that this was a special time for us. He didn't want to interrupt. But he had some news which he had to tell us. Mike noticed him first, and he gently lifted up my head and wiped away my tears.

'Jacqui, I wonder if I can talk to you for a minute?' said the doctor, when I eventually looked at him.

'Yeah, sure,' I replied hesitantly.

Mike squeezed my hand and smiled at me as I stood up. 'See you in a minute,' he said.

'Yes,' I replied.

The doctor took me into a small room down the corridor. He asked me to sit down and he hesitated before he began speaking.

'I'm sorry,' he said, 'there's no easy way to tell you this. But there is nothing anyone can do for Mike. There are some drugs we can use to alleviate his symptoms, but the only possible cure would be a heart-lung transplant and he is already too weak for that.'

He paused as I took in his words. When he could see that I wasn't ready to say anything he continued.

'I'm sorry, Jacqui. We will make him as comfortable as we can for the time that he has got left.'

'Thank you,' I said, and left the room.

Thank you? I said to myself, as I stood in the corridor looking down at the door to Mike's ward. *Thank you?* What was I thanking him for? For telling me that my husband was going to die? For letting me know that I would soon be a widow? For telling me that my whole world was about to be broken apart? And then for leaving me to go back into the ward and to pass on the news to Mike?

How did he think I could do that? Why hadn't he told Mike himself? How did he expect me to do it? I couldn't. I knew that the moment I walked back into the ward Mike would want to know what the doctor had said. How could I tell him? I couldn't.

I turned round and went the opposite way along the corridor. I ran down the stairs and out into the grounds. There was a rose garden there with paths around it and a fountain in the middle. I don't know if there was anyone else there at that time – and I didn't really care. All I wanted to do was to shout and to bawl and to scream at God.

How could he let this happen to us? It just can't be real. It can't be happening.

I don't know how long I screamed and shouted at God, but when I stopped I just sank on to the grass and sobbed.

I began to pray. 'Lord, I really need you. I can't face this on my own. I can't cope. I can't do it. I need you, Lord.'

I meet many people today who tell me that suffering shows that there is no God. I understand why they say that. I know what it is to feel hurt and angry and abandoned. I know what it feels like to be rejected and ridiculed. I know what it is to have all your hopes and dreams shattered and destroyed.

But all I can say is that my experience of suffering has proved to me that God does exist. There, in the garden, as I cried out to him, he came and he met with me. I didn't see him, of course, but I knew he was there. I didn't feel his arms around me as I had felt Mike's so many times, but I knew that he was surrounding me with his love. I knew that, whatever happened, he would never leave me. I knew that he would always be there beside me, behind me, in front of me. And I knew that, when the time came for Mike to die, God would take him into his arms and lead him up to a brighter, better place, where he would be happy, and where he could walk those heavenly hills, together with his Lord, without ever getting out of breath.

I had experienced God many times in the past few years – ever since I had become a Christian at that summer camp. But never had I known him so close. Never had I experienced him so intimately. Never had I felt him so personally.

Eventually, when I knew that I couldn't take any more of God's intense presence, I stood up and walked back into the hospital. Slowly I climbed the stairs and turned into the corridor. It was then that I noticed the doctors and nurses running past me. For a moment I didn't pay any attention to them. Until I saw that they had gone into Mike's ward. At that my heart sank and my head spun. I ran as fast as I could along the corridor. My mind raced even faster than my legs. In my mind I could see Mike lying on his bed, surrounded by the doctors and nurses, but looking for me. I could see his eyes scanning around for mine, and his hand held out, searching desperately for me to hold on to it and to comfort him. But I wasn't there. I was gone – just when he needed me most.

I reached the door and turned into the ward, to see Mike looking straight ahead at the crowd of white coats that were frantically working on the man in the opposite bed. When he saw me he began to cry. First they were little tiny drops that gently escaped from the corner of one eye. But they soon grew to large tears that were forced out by his uncontrollable sobs.

I climbed up on his bed and took his head in my arms. I didn't say anything, I just held him and stroked his hair, and cried along with him. A nurse came and drew the curtains around us. We sat in silence, listening to the sound of the man in the opposite bed as he died.

'Jacqui, what are you going to do?' Mike said, eventually.

'I'm going to stay here with you, all the time. I'm never going to leave you alone again.' I replied.

He looked up at me and smiled.

'No, Jacqui. What are you going to do when I go, when I leave you?'

'Don't. Please don't. Don't talk like that.'

'But, Jacqui, we've got to face it.'

I wanted to tell him what the doctor had said. I wanted to explain it in the clear, clinical terms he had used, but I couldn't say anything. I tried to move my lips but nothing came out.

'I'm dying, Jacqui,' he said. 'Do you know that? There's nothing they can do, I can tell. I'm not scared, you know. I'm actually quite looking forward to it – going to heaven to be with God. I can't wait to go. But I don't want to leave you. I really don't want to leave you. I'm sorry. I'm so sorry. I haven't been what you wanted, what you needed.'

'No,' I said. 'You are everything I want – everything I have always needed. Don't be sorry. I love you.'

Mike started crying again. And so did I. Our tears fell side by side and mingled on the sheets.

We sat together on that bed, with our arms entwined around one another, for many hours that night. And for the many days that followed. The nurses moved Mike into another room, where there were no other patients. That gave us more privacy – and so it was easier for Andy and Julia, and Tony and Sharon, to be with us. I really needed them around. It seemed like Mike and I were waiting in a departure lounge for a plane that would arrive some time, but we just didn't know when.

So we spent many hours together, the six of us, in that room. Waiting. Talking. It was there that we told our life-stories to one another. Mike said that he really enjoyed hearing our voices and wanted us to talk around him. He also seemed to listen to us as much as he could – in between the periods when he drifted off to sleep.

It was in that time that I found out so much about the lives my new friends had led in the past. We opened up to one another as we sat together and told our stories in that room. We shared our inner secrets and our deepest thoughts. We spoke of some things that we had never told anyone else before.

I remember looking at Andy and Sharon, in particular, and thinking how much they must have changed since they had become Christians.

There was Andy with his selfless devotion to the very difficult kids he was working with day by day. I wondered how many of the people who saw him now knew what he had been like in the past.

And there was Sharon – so peaceful and calm. I wondered how many of the people who are so touched and moved by her know of her past life. Would they believe it possible that God could change someone as much as he had changed her?

But while we talked of the past we also spoke of the future. Each of us shared our hopes and our dreams, we spoke of our deepest longings and heartfelt yearnings. In fact we were honest with one another about some of our frustrations and the things we wanted to happen in the future.

Andy had big plans to start a new business. He wanted to run some kind of commercial operation which would provide employment for people whom other employers just didn't seem to want to take on. 'There are so many people who feel as if they are on the scrap heap of life,' he said. 'They feel that they have got nothing to offer society – but they have, if we can help them to see that. I don't quite know what to do yet, but I know that I want to use my business skills to make a difference in this world. I want to do something which includes the excluded – that gives everyone a chance to know that they are important and valuable.'

The truth was that Andy was actually becoming quite frustrated with the work he was doing. He told us that he was no longer satisfied with his current job. He needed something new. He needed to move on. 'I won't really be happy until I get that new business going,' he said.

Tony and Sharon also had big plans. They wanted to move on to work in an inner-city parish. 'We want to live amongst the drug dealers and the prostitutes,' Sharon said. 'We understand them, we can relate to them – and we want to show those people that God loves them just as much as he loves everyone else.'

They, too, spoke of their unhappiness and frustration at the moment. 'We were really pleased when we first arrived,' said Tony, 'but now I know that I need to move on to an area which suits my ministry better. We won't really be happy until we get to an inner-city parish.'

I also had plans, hopes and dreams of what God would do in me and through me. But at the time I couldn't really think about them. All I could see was my world being shattered all around me.

Mike didn't talk much when the rest of us shared our life-stories together around his bed, nor while we talked about our frustrations and our search for happiness in the future. He couldn't really speak. He had become too weak.

But there was one time when he surprised us all by joining in quite suddenly.

'If only,' he said one night. They were the first words he had spoken for an hour or more. We thought he had been asleep, but he must have been listening and thinking. Perhaps when you are dying, like Mike was, you can stand back from life and get a better understanding of it.

'If only,' he said again. 'You know, you were all so alike. And you still are. Have you got it now? Or only got part of it?' I squeezed his hand and he smiled at me.

'I had a present once,' he continued. 'A cake, it was. My mum gave it to me when I was away from home for a while. But I never opened the tin until it was too late.'

At the time we couldn't figure out what he meant, or whether he really knew what he was saying. Was he delirious? Or was he thinking more clearly than any of us?

'You know what?' he continued a little while later. 'I don't say "if only" any more. I just trust God. And I enjoy each day.'

*   *   *

Just over a week later I walked down the aisle with Mike. All of our friends were there to watch and to share in it with us – just as they had been at our wedding.

Except that this time they didn't cheer, or take photos. And Mike wasn't holding my hand. He was carried by some of our closest friends.

Tony led the way as he spoke out the words: 'I am the resurrection and the life. He who believes in me, though he die, yet shall he live; and whoever lives and believes in me shall never die.'

I sat down on the front pew with Andy on one side and Julia on the other. Tony smiled at me as he led the service. And I tried to join in as much as I could.

After the second hymn, Sharon stood and took her place at the microphone. She prepared to read out a poem.

'Jacqui,' she said, 'this is for you. It's called "Hope for Today".'

The poem had been specially written for the occasion

and it came to mean so much to me in the years that followed.

But it wasn't just for me. It was for all of us who have loved and lost, for all of us whose hopes and dreams have been shattered, for all of us who say 'If only', for all of us who have to learn what it really means to trust God, day by day.

Hope for Today

There's a place deep in my heart I rarely go
It hides a memory that only we know
And an ache that on the outside doesn't show

A love was lost, a life was scarred so brutally
A wound that others rarely see
Now I'm longing for some arms to shelter me

And as the pain goes by and the memories fade
I'll trust in your love, I'll rest in your shade
Your arms of comfort will come to my aid

I won't live my life in the hopes of yesterday
'Cos the winds of change have come and blown them away

And I know the peace you bring is here, and here to stay
Though I cannot see the future
There's always hope for today

I'll walk this treadmill on my own, or so it seems
No one to care or share my dreams
But then I realise your love is holding me

And as the pain goes by and the memories fade
I'll trust in your love, I'll rest in your shade
Your arms of comfort will come to my aid

I won't live my life in the hopes of yesterday
'Cos the winds of change have come and blown them
away

And I know the peace you bring is here, and here to stay
Though I cannot see the future
There's always hope for today

Matrix Revelations
A Thinking Fan's Guide to the Matrix Trilogy
Editor Steve Couch

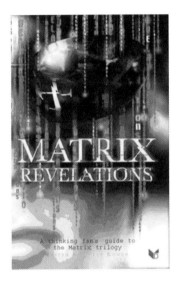

The first in the *Thinking Fan's Guide* series, providing in-depth analysis of the ideas behind the *Matrix* films written for fans of the films by fans of the films.

What is *The Matrix*?

Groundbreaking, innovative and much imitated, the *Matrix* trilogy represents the most talked about cinematic experience in recent years. Unrivalled in uniting serious philosophical thought with serious box office, *The Matrix, The Matrix Reloaded* and *The Matrix Revolutions* occupy a unique place in popular culture.

Matrix Revelations examines the *Matrix* phenomenon, with in-depth analysis ranging from the science fiction and comic book influences to the philosophical and religious themes that underpin the films.

Dark Matter
A Thinking Fan's Guide to Philip Pullman
Tony Watkins

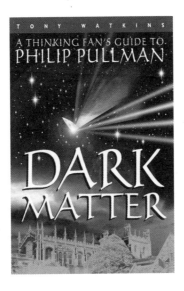

Another in the popular *Thinking Fan's Guide* series, exploring the major themes of Philip Pullman's *His Dark Materials* trilogy.

Philip Pullman's *His Dark Materials* trilogy is rightly acclaimed as a modern classic. Pullman creates alternative worlds that fascinate and delight, and has built up a loyal army of readers. He has been described as the 'most significant', but also the 'most dangerous' author in Britain. Who is Philip Pullman and why have his books provoked such a wide variety of strong opinions?

Tony Watkins explains what makes *His Dark Materials* such a magnificent work of fiction. He explores the influences that shaped Pullman's writing and the major themes of the trilogy, including demons, Dust and Pullman's perspective on God.

I Wish I Could Believe in Meaning
Peter S. Williams

Peter S. Williams digs beneath our sceptical culture and invites us to take time out from the 'party' to seriously consider some of life's big questions – about truth, knowledge, goodness and beauty. He builds a convincing case for belief in meaning and purpose. In critiquing the arguments of zoologist Richard Dawkins he presents a serious challenge to naturalism. This book offers an alternative to atheism that addresses some of our deepest questions about life.

Teenagers: Why Do They Do That?
Nick Pollard

Concerned about teen drug-taking, pregnancies and eating disorders? Baffled about what drives many teenagers to such behaviour? Worried that 'it must be my fault'?

This brilliantly enlightening book argues that understanding the culture in which teenagers are growing up is the key to understanding why some inflict tragedy upon themselves or others.

Nick Pollard, a specialist in teenage spiritual and moral education, provides adults with invaluable insights to enable them to open doors of communication with teenagers and begin to influence them for good.